VOICES OF NEBRASKA

VOICES OF
NEBRASKA

DIVERSE LANDSCAPES, DIVERSE PEOPLES

Edited by the Staff of the University of Nebraska Press

University of Nebraska Press | Lincoln & London

Library of Congress Control Number: 2016951036

Designed and set in Whitman by L. Auten.

PRIZE WINNERS

Poetry	Thaddeus Simpson and Daniel McIlhon
Nonfiction	Lane Chasek
Fiction	Catherine Pedigo and Kristi Walsh

CONTENTS

Water Girls 1
NINA HJERMSTAD

The Adventures of a Beautiful Life 9
BRIANNA AGUILAR

A Farmer's Life 15
ASHLEY LYNNE COOK

My Little Slice of the Good Life 17
RACHEL DANIELSON

Rusty Cars 21
ALEXIS VRANA

"For Nebraska,"
"Lyrics to Jimmy's Song, the Lockjaws 2013,"
and "Building Limestone Fathers" 27
THADDEUS SIMPSON

The Backdrop of My Biography   35
KAMRIN BAKER

Becoming Vegan in Western Nebraska   39
LANE CHASEK

Hatchet House   47
LUKE GILBERT

My Dad Is Dead   57
AMANDA HOVSETH

"Living Statues on Highway 77,"
"Spectators of Nebraska,"
and "Memory Keepers of Waverly"   71
SARA MOSIER

Road to Redemption   75
BRIANA DAVIS

Cottonwood   87
CATHERINE PEDIGO

"Some Autumn Holiday,"
"When It Happens,"
and "The Main Street Fair"   99
DANIEL MCILHON

Reefer Madness   105
ALEXA WALKER

The Search for Her   117
FAITH VICTORIA TRACY

The Genuine Effect   121
BRIAN POMPLUN

Release   127
KRISTI WALSH

There Is No Place Like Nebraska   145
ELLIE FEIS

Contributors   149

VOICES OF NEBRASKA

Water Girls

NINA HJERMSTAD

I watch my mom when she thinks I'm not looking. She hunches over the hard-water-stained sink, crunching her little yellow pills to dust like they're Smarties. The doctor prescribed two. When it looked like we weren't getting to the pharmacy anytime soon, she rationed herself to one.

"Just until the police come," she said. Or the government or God or whoever was supposed to save us. Looks like she gave up on that.

"Rhi! Rhi-rhi-rhi-rhi-rhi!" Flea grabs my hand and bounces. Mom looks up, and our eyes lock in the murky glass of the medicine cabinet.

I cling to Flea's chubby hand and wheel her around the corner. "What? What do you want?" I whisper-shout.

"Take me to see the water girls." Flea stamps her foot, then, remembering what I told her about being bossy, "Please?"

I sigh. The image comes unbidden. Girls, women in long, flowing dresses in a rainbow of shades floating in the floodwater below the apartment complex. They never seem to puff up or rot like I expect them to. They glide gently as if there were a current in the stagnant water or like they were being guided by magnets deep in the earth. Their dresses and hair glow in the darkness as they lifelessly drift on the flooded first floor of the Cuddle Inn. Flea begs me every day to watch them from the stairwell. They remind her of mermaids. Can't get much more messed up than that.

"No. Not now." Not ever.

Flea screws up her little face at me and squints her eyes. Radioactive green. Every inch of her oozes a bit of sickly, jaundiced light. If it's true what they say about kids being like sponges, then my sister is a walking chunk of yellow cake uranium.

I can see the tantrum coming on, a little chemical flicker in her alien baby features. "No, Flea don't!"

"Mooooooooommmmmmm!!! Rhi is being mean to me!"

I hear the medicine cabinet slam. "For Christ's sake, Rhiannon! Get her out of this fucking room! I can't even hear myself think."

My mother moves like an animal now, or some cannibal with the shakes. She twitches a lot, and her teeth are rotting out of her face. If I told you she was pretty before all this, I'd be lying. Ever see *The Shining*? That butterface bitch, Wendy? Yeah, she could have been Mom's twin. If anything, the apocalypse agrees with her. At least she has a bit of a glow now.

I guess that means I'm ugly too. Every time I look in the mirror I see the same girl I was before the world went to shit. Pale skin, dark hair (ponytailed), and purple hoodie. My skin hasn't sagged or gone gray or oozed glow-stick yellow pus. *Maybe*, I always think to myself, *maybe I'm immune*.

Immune to the apocalypse, that is. Not to my mother's bullshit.

"Do you even know what you're asking me to do? You want me to take your daughter to go see some dead girls float around in toilet water? Can your drug-addled brain understand how fucked up that is?"

Mom practically hisses at me; the gunk in her lungs gargles in the back of her throat like tonic, and a bit of drool bubbles from the side of her mouth. She moves at me in a flash, and in that nanosecond before she smacks me with her crusty skeleton hand I can see Old Mom dancing in the kitchen to Heart and Stevie Nicks, making chocolate chip pancakes for dinner because life is short. My ear is ringing from where she clubbed it, and I hear the crackle of our old radio like a warm campfire.

Will you ever win? Will you ever win? Rhiannon . . .

Mom bites deep into the soft, pale flesh of Old Mom's throat and rips out a mess of cords and cables. Dead.

I scoop up my sister. "C'mon, Flea. Let's get away from this raving bitch." "Water girls! Water girls!" she chants.

She's the most selfish child I've ever met, honestly.

I carry her up all eleven flights of stairs to the hotel's roof. I tell myself I'm getting stronger and that soon I'll be able to get out of here. A few smog-covered pigeons wheel in the sky.

"Fishy, fishy, fishy! Come down and see Flea!" she calls up to them and waves her bulbous little fingers in the sky.

"They're birds, dummy. And they're not coming down." I spent weeks trying to catch them. Nets, pots and pans, I even used some of our precious bread crumbs to try and lure them out of the sky. I spent whole nights and days without sleep, without ever coming back to our room, waiting for the damn pigeons to give up and fall out of the sky. On those nights, I looked up at the blinking fluorescent stars and wondered if the dinosaurs ever felt like I did then.

Flea's screaming intensifies out of nowhere. Doctors and teachers called her a "troubled child" before. She's batshit crazy now. She's leaning so far over the edge, it could hardly be my fault. A strong wind could do it, but I don't know if I have the patience to wait. Besides, there hasn't been more than a dry whisper in the air in days. My hands are on her, and I rock forward with her. I sniff deep, and the little curls of air tickle the scabs inside my nostrils and fill my body with a strong wind, like we are tumbling over the edge, scraping against the polluted sky to the earth below.

I rock back on my heels and hug her to me. Not yet. Not just yet.

There's something beautiful about our suite-style room. Honestly, I think I just hated it so much when we first got here that it makes me happy to see it destroyed. It was stuffy and starchy, like an abandoned hospital turned into a bed and breakfast. Ugly floral curtains and bedspreads lie flat against the room, stiff and cold, while chintzy fabric flowers wither and gather dust on the table that smells like it's been in storage with old women and their armada of pissing cats. The quilts have been stripped off the beds and are lying in a tangled, dirty mass like a pile of bodies on the floor. Mom and I put up corrugated metal sheets in front of the windows, and stray beams of light dance through from where the acid rain chewed them to rust. I like the room now. It's like walking into a diorama made by a third grader. Scraps of fabric, dirt, holes poked in the side for stars. When the red sun struggles across the sky and squats down on the horizon, I feel an animal beauty revel in me. I want to dance and spin in the room between the ribbons of light, jump and pirouette like a baton twirler and chant Native American songs.

Maybe one day I will. I'll paint my naked, bony body with soot and some of Flea's lava-lamp blood and dance like a goddess of death around my mother's decrepit body. The thought of it gives me chills. The good kind. I close my eyes for a minute and savor the orgasmic little goosebumps crawling over my ghostly skin. I feel like I've been dunked in Sprite or fancy champagne and I'm being washed with life. Kitten sneezes and children's laughter.

There's a clatter in the kitchenette, and air rushes by my face and rustles my eyelashes. I feel like a rocket took off in front of me. I hear ragged breathing, feel the heat pulsating off her heaving chest. I won't open my eyes this time. I'll just stand here until I fall asleep or die, whichever comes first. She takes my hand in her scabby one, and I feel her pull close to me, her thin lips molding bumpy words and tickling my ear.

"She rings like a bell through the night and wouldn't you love to love her? She rules her life like a bird in flight and who will be her lover?"

Her lips are on mine, cold and flat, flat, flat. I open my eyes and see my own in the clouds in the glass of the medicine cabinet, little whirlpools of another world.

I see Mom and Flea at the water's edge, and bright light flashes in my mind like the static-y barrier between distant radio stations. Sunlight, sand, Mom in a floppy hat and retro one-piece, her arm around a pig-tailed Flea, laughing at the ocean. Darkness, a naked, flickering bulb in the distance, two unrecognizable forms dressed in rags. Little bubbles flicker on the surface where Flea ends and the water begins.

"Hush, baby. Drink it in. You're one of the pretty water girls now."

My sweaty fingers lick the reptilian flesh of the pistol's grip; it feels like I'm holding hands with a robot's claw on a first date.

Click. Safety off. *Exhale.* Aim. *Pow.*

Mom flops into the water like a diabetic Free Willy, and little Flea bobs away down the hall.

I can't stand the dark anymore. I feel my blind eyes blacken and shrivel in my head every second I stay. Shattered bits of poetry from another world stab my brain. *Do not go gentle into that good night.* I push my feet up the stairs, wheezing with each step. *Rage, rage against the dying of the light.*

On my way to the balcony, I catch a reflection of myself in the dented toaster. I finally see it.

"Oh, Jesus," I sob. I clutch the toaster with shaking hands and wipe away the gunk with my sleeve. I look like that creepy little guy in *Lord of the Rings.* My head is mostly bald and scabby with the occasional patch of stringy, greasy black hair. My cheeks are sunken in, and my eyes stick out like I'm being squeezed. Something about the pupils is very wrong. They don't look human anymore. The skin and tissue on the end of my nose is flaking off in such big chunks that it is beginning to disfigure me. My lips are huge and chapped with a colony of angry, puckered sores around the edges. I moan, and the sound comes to my poisoned ears like an injured animal.

Sooty tears stain my pointy cheeks. I throw the toaster hard at the wall and terrify myself with the giant sound in the crushing silence.

I had planned to be looking over the balcony when I did it. I was going to do one last check to see if I was the only person alive. The only living, breathing, remorse-feeling human left in this big goddamn wasteland of a world. I close my tired eyes and see Flea's little body floating among the remains of a successful suicide pact. Human. I lie down on the jagged tile floor and see myself sideways in the toaster one last time. Human? I could never be human again. I put the cool metal pipe between my lips and close my eyes to taste it. It tastes like my first kiss.

Taken by, taken by the sky . . .

"Oh Jesus, Al." The officer clapped a hand over his nose. "Je-sus Christ." He retched, and his sub sandwich crawled up his throat, using his windpipe as a foothold.

Sergeant Al Benson shook his head and scoffed, taking in the scene. "And here I was thinking Nebraska was boring. A few speeding tickets, some DUIs. Nothing but corn and cows and girls that look like they'd fuck either." His wiry mustache bristled when he smiled, and he rubbed it as if he could wipe away the stench of rotting human. "Well, I'll be damned. This is a goddamn regular LA crime scene."

The young officer returned to Al's side, shaking. "What . . . what am I even seeing?"

"Well," Al hiked up his suspenders and snapped them back into place on his sweat-patched shirt, "over here you've got this young miss, got her brains all over the kitchen." He made a tsk-ing sound. "And if you follow me . . ." Al sauntered with his usual cowboy-style gait and pushed open the door to the bathroom. The smell amplified ten-fold. "Here we have two more ladies, the little one drowned in the tub and the older one—" Al pulled the body up by the back of the collar, "looks like she got clipped in the back of the dome."

The two men stood silently at the edge of a splatter of blood, the drops reflecting in their freshly polished loafers. "Water pollution," Al murmured.

"What?"

Al lifted his hat and rubbed his balding scalp. "Ever heard of the Salem witch trials, son?"

"Sure. I guess so."

"LSD comes from ergot. Ergot is this weird fungus shit in rye. Ergot can get in water too."

"Oh, Jesus . . ."

"Those girls weren't witches. The whole town was just trippin' balls."

"I thought this place was closed months ago?"

"Yeah, well, people like this," Al nudged the woman's body with the toe of his shoe, "people like this always go where they're not wanted."

The Adventures of
a Beautiful Life

BRIANNA AGUILAR

In the early 1900s, the Mexican Revolution hit the city of Leon Guanajuato so devastatingly that Juan Palomares sent away his wife, Abundia Ramirez, and their kids to America—although this story is much more complicated and intriguing than that due to Juan's friendship with one man. The relationship Juan and his family had with Pancho Villa was taking a nasty turn. Villa was on a massive recruiting spree to build his army for the Revolution, and he wanted Juan and his sons. Juan was not going to let this happen to his family, so he sent his wife and kids away to ensure their safety and freedom while he stayed behind to fight. He told them that when things settled down and the war was over, he would call them back to their home. They waited for months, then years, then a century, and never heard from him again. There is still no record of what happened to Juan.

Their daughter Isabelle Ramirez was around the age of twenty and married with four children. When her husband, Jacinto Gomez, learned of her family's leaving, he told her to go and assured her that he would catch up. He tried for months to get across the border, but the guards never let him. His good buddy Jacinto Aguilar (who, oddly enough, looked identical to Jacinto Gomez) was able to cross the border legally. So one day Jacinto Gomez lied, saying his name was Jacinto Aguilar, and used his friend's name and identification to successfully make it across the border and safely to his family. Legally, the name Aguilar had to stick.

The family found work not too long after they settled in Grand Island, Nebraska. Leo Stuhr took them under his wing and gave them work in the beet fields. Not too long after, Abundia Ramirez gave up hope of hearing from her husband and peacefully died. In the year 1934, Seraphine Aguilar was born on August 25, in Grand Island. Growing up, Seraphine worked with his family in the beet fields, but he was mostly just the water boy and taco boy as a young child. Of Leo Stuhr he said, "He was a good man, such a good man, and always treated us with respect and had always cared for us. He was a very rich man and had so much money that he didn't know what to do with it! He never married and had no children, so we were his family. He used to bring us big bags of candy at the end of each week, and my gosh, it felt like Christmas!"

Jacinto worked for the railroad, while the rest of his family worked in the beet fields. When Seraphine was around the age of five, Jacinto and Isabelle divorced, leaving Isabelle with nine kids to provide for. He never kept in touch, so the family didn't know where he was or what happened to him until he died of old age around the year 1969. Leo was a very good man to the whole family, allowing Isabelle to have four jobs. She worked as a maid at the Yancey Hotel, as a waitress at the Central Cafe, for Mr. Leo, and she also worked at the Saint Francis Hospital in the laundry room.

Throughout the years, Leo was a teacher to Seraphine and taught him how to read and write. But when Seraphine reached the age of nine or ten, Leo found a good school to enroll him in. In high school at the age of sixteen, Seraphine was approached by an officer who talked him into joining the military. He knew it was something he could never pass up. So he lied about his age and was enrolled in the service for four years. He fought in the Korean War and the Vietnam War. "It was one of the most horrific times of my life. The war taught me to appreciate and to love. Still today I have the horrid pictures floating around in my mind, and those times of my life are just something I will never forget," Seraphine tells of his experiences.

Every five months, he would send money to his mother to help her support the rest of his family. When released from the service and with the money he had saved over the years, he took his mother and their family back to Mexico where Isabelle had been raised. The day they arrived in Leon Guanajuato, Isabelle broke down in tears. All the villages and farms had been completely wiped away; her home was no longer her home, and the memories were suddenly only a vision of a past life she once loved. She had no idea which direction was which because it was like a whole different country to her. Disappointed and disgruntled, the family came back to Grand Island to move on with their lives and establish a new beginning. Five years later, Isabelle died of influenza. "When my mother died, I felt like I died with her. I couldn't ever imagine a life without her," Seraphine elaborated on the death of his mother.

Seraphine moved to Hastings, Nebraska, and found a job in a printing shop. There, he worked for four years and got his printership in 1955. He continued his work in Hastings and also held a job in Grand Island at Skagway for eighteen years. In 1962 Seraphine fell in love and married a woman named Donna Hayes; they had their first child, Tony, on April 16. A couple years later, on August 17, 1964, they had another boy named Alan. Their final child was yet another boy, Rico, born on September 7, 1972. When Rico was just under a year old, Donna fled, leaving Seraphine to care for their three boys. Nothing was ever heard from her again. Around the year of 1974, Seraphine opened a printing business of his own, located on Fourth Street. Not only that, but he traveled around Nebraska as a singer and sang karaoke. You could say Seraphine did pretty well for himself over the years.

A few years after the printing business opened, he married one of his workers, Dianne Hart, on November 4, 1976. They had two kids of their own and cared for the other three boys as well. Their first child was a boy, born on January 6, 1975, named Mario Aguilar. He grew up to look and be just like his father, inside and out. Mario later fell madly in love with a woman named Staci Hawke. At the age of twenty-two, they had their first child on January 22, 1998, a little girl, Brianna Aguilar. Although identical to her mother, she is lucky to have the heart of both of her parents. Two years later, they had their second child on July 17, 2000, another little girl, who is now all grown up into a young woman. Not too long after, the family finally had a little boy in their lives on May 23, 2003. He has grown up to be the sweetest and most tender-hearted kid, and luckily enough, he looks just like his oldest sister.

Seraphine and Dianne's second child was a girl, Maria Aguilar, born on September 8, 1979. She married the love of her life, Chad Tibbetts, on May 14, 2005, and they had three little girls. The first child was named Ana Tibbetts and was born on November 15, 2006. The other two girls look identical to their mother. The second child was born July 31, 2008, and received the name Elle Tibbetts. The third daughter is so ornery but also a big heart warmer. She was born on August 22, 2010, and named Eva. She is usually referred to as "Eva the Diva" because of that wonderful ornery trait she carries around. Leave it to these beauties to put a warm smile on your face.

If you're wondering where the rest of Seraphine's siblings are today, you won't find too much. They all passed away due to old age, and the only two standing are Seraphine and his older sister Mary, who is only a couple years older than he is.

Seraphine is so inspirational because the stories he shares are so thrilling and astonishing! His grandparents and parents came from Mexico because of the Mexican Revolution, and they all had to find work to help support themselves. Seraphine joined the military to help his mother support the family and then raised enough money to take her back to where she grew up, only to find that their beloved home was gone. Each family member took on multiple jobs and responsibilities to get by. It's hard for us to be selfish with the things we have when we look at our family's history and see all of the obstacles they had to overcome that we never had to. Through all the hardships and struggles that Seraphine and his family faced, they all turned out with loving families, and that's all you need to have a beautiful life.

BIBLIOGRAPHY

Aguilar, Seraphine. Personal interview, October 18, 2015.

A Farmer's Life

ASHLEY LYNNE COOK

I rise before the sun,
to accomplish what needs to be done.
In order to survive on this earth,
to nurture the fruits of worth.
From the sea of golden grains,
to the beasts that roam these plains.
Where my hopes and dreams dwell,
when only time will tell.
Pouring my heart and soul into the soil,
with the struggle of my lifelong toil.

My Little Slice of
the Good Life

RACHEL DANIELSON

My sister, Leah, shook me awake before the sun had started its trek above the horizon. I stretched to loosen the sleep from my bones before my big sister helped me get dressed. In the kitchen, Grandpa sat at the table sipping his coffee while Grandma banged through the cupboards, starting breakfast.

She looked up. "How'd you sleep, honey?" "Goooood."

My always ornery cousin, David, caught her eye. "David Robert, stop playing with that lighter and go get dressed. Breakfast will be ready in a minute."

He threw down the lighter and slid back from the table. Grandma breathed a sigh of relief. She had become slightly leery of David around fire after he had used a can of hairspray and a lighter to make a flamethrower in the middle of the kitchen.

A small while later, he emerged from his bedroom and joined Leah, Grandpa, and me at the table. We sat and ate, just following our typical morning routine whenever I stayed at my grandparents' farm, before heading out to help with the chores. Leah, David, and

I all piled into the truck with Grandpa to help start the irrigation. We bounced down the dirt roads, sending up dust to mix with the palette of colors splashing across the Nebraska sky. Turning off into the field's side roads, the bumps really started to pick up, so of course, all of us kids had to send out the steady hum of our voices and laugh when the washboard of the roads reverberated through our throats. *Ughl-Ughl-Ughl-Ughl-Ughl.* Grandpa joined in with us until he pulled his truck to a stop in the tunnels of corn. Leah grabbed my hand, and we scattered from David and Grandpa, each knowing our job. Leah leaned over the mound of dirt and tapped open the spigots of the pipes along the lines of corn, sending a crystal flow of water cascading down the dirt rows.

After all of the irrigation was started in the corn and bean fields, we headed back to the farm. It was our job to gather the eggs while Grandpa fed the rest of the animals. We snuck into the hen house among the clucks of the chickens, reaching under their warm feathers to grab their eggs.

Once we had gathered the eggs, we walked back to the house, twisting under the trees along the road. The act of handing the eggs to Grandma meant we were free for the rest of the day. Until evening chores, anyway.

The three of us ran around the property, jumping in the scratchy hay, climbing trees, building forts, and riding the four-wheelers with me clutching to my sister's back like a koala.

We were in our tree house when we heard Grandma's voice in the distance calling us in for supper. We scurried down the tree and ran to the house, signifying the end of another glorious summer day.

The moment I awoke, I knew. The first snowfall of winter had finally come. I jumped out of bed and ran down the hall. I pressed against the window and gazed at the blanket of white covering my world until the fog on the window persuaded me to the dining room, where my mother sat.

"Mom! Can we go sledding?"

A smile touched her lip. "After Leah wakes up."

"Well, can I go wake her up?"

"No. Eat some breakfast. She'll be up shortly."

"Fiiine."

I grabbed a bowl and started pouring some cereal, obviously not trying to be quiet. "Rachel Lois, you better not wake up your sister."

I sighed, disappointed my infallible plan had been ruined. However, it didn't take long for Leah to finally awake. And it definitely didn't take long for us to dig our snow clothes out of the closet.

After Mom inspected our clothing to ensure we were properly covered, she cleared us for the outside world. Leah and I tumbled out the door and slid across the deck. Climbing up onto the railing, we jumped into a drift of snow before heading to the shed to dig out the sled.

Our trusty red sleds gleamed against the white backdrop as they trailed behind us. We eagerly climbed the sand piles behind our house.

Leah positioned her sled at the top of the hill.

And I protested, "How's come you always get to go first?"

She sighed and looked back at me. "Because I have to blaze the trail first. That way you'll go faster and have more fun." She plopped down on the sled. "And you won't get hurt."

My sister. My watchful guardian and playmate. Even with four years between us, she had always been my best friend.

She slowly plowed through the thick blanket of snow, leaving a packed trail behind her just like she promised.

She reached the bottom. "Okay, now you go!"

I grinned, threw myself onto the hard surface of the sled, and pushed off. I flew down the hill. The cold air bit at my exposed skin, and flakes of snow flew up into the air, swirling around me. Joy coursed through me.

I reached the bottom laughing. Rolling out of the sled, I buried my face in the snow and licked some up. The ice-cold flakes melted across my tongue.

"Let's go again!"

After we had worn out every hill sledding, we decided to build a snowman, which of course led to a snowball fight. We played the whole day, outside in the glittering snow with our breath curling around as we filled the air with laughter.

Every Nebraska kid knows the pure joy that arrives with the first snowfall.

"What do you wanna do?" I asked as I rocked in the porch swing. "I don't know. What'd you wanna do?" Leah answered.

I gave her a look and finished out our favorite scene from *The Jungle Book*, "Don't start that again."

She laughed and jumped down from the railing of our deck. "Let's go fishing."

We slipped inside the house to tell Mom where we were going before setting off down the road with our bags and poles in hand. The hot, humid air pressed in around us. A bead of sweat trickled down my forehead. I wiped it away. "Can we go swimming too, Leah?"

"Yeah, after we catch a few fish."

"Okay."

We left the main road that wrapped around our property and traveled down the tire-track trail that cut through the tall grass and sunflowers. The cottonwoods danced and released puffs of cotton like snow whenever a hot breath of wind came. The sandpit came into view, dazzling in the July sunshine. Pumped straight out of the Nebraska sand bordering the Platte River, our sandpit had become my favorite place in the whole world with its clear blue-green water and buzzing dragonflies. Leah and I walked down the incline, sand flicking up into our flip-flops, to the paddleboat resting on the bank. We threw our stuff in before gliding it out onto the cool water.

Casting and feeling the occasional tug on the line, we fished until the heat became unbearable. I stood up and slid off my shoes right as Leah pushed me into the water. Sweet relief, yet shocking. I came up for air and grabbed her arm, pulling her in with me. Laughter joined the chorus of the birds' songs.

Rusty Cars

ALEXIS VRANA

I had known Harold my entire life. Out of all my dad's friends, Harold was my family's favorite one. He owned a car repair shop, full of old cars, trucks, and tractors. The shop was in such a peaceful place—that is until a train flew by blaring its horn. The smell of old rusty cars always filled my nostrils as I hopped out of my dad's pickup truck and ran toward the shop to greet Harold and his dog.

Harold's attire was one of the things that made him memorable. His old ratty jeans, holey plaid shirts, dirty hat, and sneakers covered in grease stains made him noticeable anywhere he went. He wore glasses from the '70s and had long, brown, stringy hair. The thing I remember most about Harold was his long, brown, wiry beard. He appeared as though he were lost in a time warp and didn't have two dimes to rub together.

When my sister, Evann, and I were small children, my dad took us out to Harold's shop all the time; we ran around with Harold's dog, Brownie. He was a mutt with short brown hair and white spots. When Brownie became bored with us, my sister and I loved jumping off and climbing under Harold's old rusty Volkswagen Beetles. Harold and my dad watched us and laughed as they shared their own random conversations.

Harold shared so many funny and insightful stories and experiences. He always said, "You should never look good when you go to barter for something—it's better if they think you're poor." At Pioneer Village once, a child thought Harold was part of the exhibit because he was so still and intent on studying something, and of course, he was dressed in his worn, outdated outfit with his beard and long hair. Harold once lost money in a savings and loan, so he had no faith in banks. He kept his money in untraditional places stashed all around his properties. When he passed away, they found money in a variety of places, including the pockets of clothes in his closet and in a rundown old house that he owned.

Harold had hundreds of cars in various stages of repair or disrepair. My dad made the mistake of calling it "junk" once. Harold corrected him. "It's not junk, it's inventory." Harold knew where everything in his shop was even though it looked like a mess to visitors. He even had an old airplane in his "inventory." Despite the appearance of his shop, Harold "knew" cars. He helped my dad restore an old 1947 Ford truck that my great-grandfather had owned, and we still love to ride around in it today.

One day my dad sat me down and told me that Harold was sick. I wasn't too concerned because he didn't seem sick. It wasn't until I noticed the lack of energy and the pain he was in that it actually hit me. This man I had known my entire life had cancer, and his chances of beating it weren't good, especially because he refused traditional treatment because he didn't trust doctors. It hurt so much to see him begin to fail. The pain got worse, and he couldn't go to his shop anymore. Finding a chair for him to sit in at our house became difficult because his pain was so severe. How could someone seem so healthy one day and then go on such a downward spiral? It soon became clear that the time we would get to spend with him was coming to an end, and I wondered why I hadn't spent more time with him. Why did I ever turn down Dad's invitations to go to Harold's shop?

When my dad brought Harold over to the house for the first time after he was diagnosed with cancer, it took every ounce of my self-control not to cry. It was tough to see somebody who was normally a fun-loving, story-telling guy being reserved and quiet. As time passed that night, Harold started warming up and becoming his normal self. He laughed and joined in with my family's conversations. When Harold was around, the conversation jumped from one subject to another, and there was no such thing as a "boring" conversation. This was a huge relief to me and my family. I'll always remember that night and how much joy and laughter Harold brought to our family when he spent time at our house.

My dad invited Harold to start coming to church with us. My sister and I were happy about this. Every Sunday, Dad left the house forty minutes early so he would have time to get Harold out of his house and into the church. By now, it was difficult for Harold to walk. He was constantly in pain, and he struggled moving his legs and lower body, but as the weeks passed, Harold's faith grew. He spent a lot of time reading the Bible with my dad and my pastor. Soon after Harold started attending Calvary Church, he was baptized. Harold's growing faith taught me a lot. I remember him saying to my dad, "Steve, I'm not scared to die anymore." That day and the smile on Harold's face have been burned into my memory. After his baptism, Harold smiled more and seemed to be happy with his life, even though it was coming to an end.

The Sunday after Harold's baptism, we planned to have him over for lunch. My mom and I went home after church to prepare the food. By the time Harold got out of the church and to the house, the food was cold, and he was too exhausted to make it inside, so we improvised. Mom and I heated up the food in the microwave while Dad set lawn chairs up in the driveway around the passenger side of his pickup. We each made our own plate of food, and I made Harold's. Out the door we went to sit and eat in lawn chairs on the driveway. I bet we looked like a bunch of fools, but that was the most memorable lunch I've ever eaten. It's the only picnic we've ever had on our driveway!

As Harold's condition worsened, Dad spent at least five nights a week with him. They spent their time driving around and talking about life. Dad was Harold's chauffeur through most of his illness, taking him to doctor visits and just driving around to get him out of his house. I occasionally rode along. Harold would talk about his insane family. He told us stories about how his sisters used to beat him up and make him do their chores. He said one of his sisters asked him for five hundred dollars a month to feed one hundred cats; he received nothing in return from her, but he sent her the money because she was his sister. He may have complained to us, but his actions taught me that no matter what, family is family, so we should love and support them in all circumstances.

Harold's death taught me a lot more about my life than I expected. I learned that I should always live the life I want to live because I never know when my world is going to come crashing down. Harold forged his own unique path and might have been judged by some as odd, but he lived his life his own way.

Harold taught me to love my family even when I don't want to or if they are living in a way that I don't approve of. His family was difficult, but he spoke of them with love and respect, and his actions toward them were generous and kind.

The way my dad treated Harold taught me so much about compassion. I learned to be giving of my time and to love and serve unconditionally. Anyone would be lucky to have a friend like my dad, and I hope to be a friend like that someday.

I was also reminded that people aren't always what they seem to be, so I shouldn't judge them by their appearance. Harold was a wise, fascinating, and successful person—he died a wealthy man, but I would never have known that from his appearance, his humble home, the shape of his shop, or the cars he drove. He was an intelligent person whose interesting life had given him an amazing perspective that most people missed because they judged him before they got beyond the long hair, beard, and old-fashioned glasses.

Harold, rest in peace.

For Nebraska

Lyrics to Jimmy's Song, the Lockjaws 2013

Building Limestone Fathers

THADDEUS SIMPSON

Panel-selected prize winner in poetry

For Nebraska

In the backwoods
where the young go to find stick swords,
in a ravine with slick, glassy water
and haunted garbage,

that's when I first saw you naked.
My reality finally unashamed.
All the city flirting,
all the cute streets and highways
they were just strings of thread for your gown
a garment meant to encourage
questions and compliments
or so I thought.

I saw your glance as an invitation,
way back when.
It's taken me all these years to realize that
you are the mother who never loved me.
You would have let me dance with the drainage
in that backwood valley,
fall face-first into that puddle
and rise,
wet, hypodermic needles clinging to my face.

But not a tear of rain would have hit your cheek.

It's not a crime to be indifferent,
I guess
I was just expecting more
after Paul Bunyan and Pocahontas
built you up to be the maiden of the West.

I first crawled down your muddy hill
to find that warmth
your hot breath
your dusty cinnamon.

But you smelled like cigarettes
and you taste like gravel.
And every bit of you
that I pull from your body
is cold and mangled and damp.
Your soil isn't the hot blood I expected.

Maybe you died before I could meet you,
it feels like I'm talking to a corpse.
But you can't be dead
your apathy is fresh.

Something still stirs
the sand beneath me
and it doesn't care what I know about it.

Lyrics to Jimmy's Song, the Lockjaws 2013

While we drank and drank
the summer shrank
and Ridley caught the blues

as long as we could keep it up
we'd all ignore the news

Ridley, Sydney, me, and Scott
Omaha's young liberal band

we played our hearts out
every night
for only a single fan

Jimmy

he was desperate to be part of us
desperate to have friends

new to the
west Omaha
grunge punk
singer plan

why'd this Sunday Schoolboy
fall in with such a crowd

did he like the dirty atmosphere
or just like bad music loud

it was Ridley who'd invited him
by complete accident

he was wandering round
the oakview mall
when she walked out hot topic

flyers flyers everywhere
she told him of our gig

the railroad tracks and overpass
was where "The Lockjaws" lived

she'd told
half a dozen
other midwest pawns and freaks

and compared to them
in Levi jeans
Jimmy was just a geek

but it was him alone
who turned up
and us four couldn't turn him back

that was months ago
and since then
he's really joined the pack

boy don't fall in love with dying
is what his mother said

I don't wanna hear the phone call
telling me you're dead

he drove the van
spray-painted black
for us
wild restless souls

I led him from the backseat
and we glided past
street poles

but smoke filled up the cabin air
so thick Jimmy couldn't see

and the elevated road didn't care
it stood in apathy

September ice
it slid us off
the dodge express
way

and for forty feet
we fell down screaming
to meet our lover's gaze

was Jimmy in love with dying
who knows
but now he's dead

were we in love with dying
maybe it was all
just in our heads

Building Limestone Fathers

On Monument island,
where pillars of generals and
philosophers stand knee-deep in hillsides,
a man hikes in the shadows cast.

His is the path of shifting gravel
beneath which lies an unstable world,
and yet how steadily the stone figures
stand above him

they must be entrenched in the planet's mantle,
their feet nailed to Earth's iron core.
as he goes traveling by.
they don't so much as flinch at him,

Were they ever really men at all?
Maybe, they were Gods,
who like the brass Achilles,
had their molten fire
drained from their heels.

Night washes over the island,
and seven-story explorers block out the stars.
The moon becomes a carpenter's halo.

Beneath a pair of wrestling giants,
the lone man sets a fire, too weak to
last a full night of ocean wind.
There are no trees on the island,
the only kindling is dried driftwood,
left on the beach like garbage,
and that burns fast.

In the orange light of the next morning,
his breakfast is an egg
eaten as raw as he found it.

After half a day more,
His journey to the other end
of the isle is finished.
There, the rocks are smaller
and so must be sculpted to a finer scale.

There aren't many good rocks left,
he must be sure to choose his own
carefully.

The Backdrop of My Biography

KAMRIN BAKER

We don't get to choose our homes.

They choose us.

Nebraska picked me when I was just a seven-month-old baby living in Naperville, Illinois. I didn't have a say whatsoever, and it's not because I was only speaking gibberish. My father's job relocated us, and my family had the option to move to Omaha, Dallas, or Seattle. My mother, being a liberal woman who doesn't like rain, allowed Nebraska to take us in—crying baby, Cornhusker-indifferent, and all.

The first ten years of my existence in one of the infamous flyover states were years of typical development in the Millard Public school district. I decorated Valentine's boxes for February 14th every year in elementary school, I walked in step through the same neighborhood with my parents and my leashed Labrador retrievers, and I smiled when the sun came out every morning.

When I was in the sixth grade, my parents got divorced. I no longer believed what the valentines said, the sidewalk suddenly became full of cracks, and sleeping was my new life passion. I wasn't aware that one day I'd have a part-time job at Hallmark, bask unbelievingly upon the dog-walking paths, and set the alarm for 6 a.m. meditations. All I knew was that life sucked, and being eleven and depressed was a task that I simply was not getting paid enough to undertake.

My mom, still a lovely constant in my life, consistently told me that as soon as I could, I would leave "this one-horse town." At that ripe of an age with that malleable of a brain, I was sold. The only thought passing my mind was that the distance between Harrison and Maple was a prison, and I was trapped in the pain of being a child of a loveless marriage. In hindsight, it was ignorant and close-minded to be so negative about my living situation, but I also know that at the time, I knew nothing more than the indescribable paralysis that I called Nebraska.

Those feelings were valid, that pain was real, and that trapped feeling was not made up. It took the attempt to write a novel and the passing of one of my friends, Anna Lundberg, my freshman year of high school for me to realize that living in this state, and just living itself, were not bad things. Simple as that. Life is good. Love is good. And we deserve both.

I figured that facing tragedy and mental illness would bulk up my strength for the years to come, and while those experiences definitely allowed me to grow and change, they did not do nearly enough. I joined the yearbook staff at Millard West, created some of the best work I've ever had the chance to conceive, signed on as a teen blogger for the *Huffington Post*, and learned how to drive. In that mesmerizing progress, however, a new sense of fever engulfed me. One day in February of my sophomore year, when I was apparently too old to be handing out candies and boxed cards professing my love, I essentially did the opposite and ended up on the floor of the nurse's office convulsing in fear. Two endless days later, I was diagnosed with a severe panic disorder.

Sleep was out of the question. Eating was impossible. Sitting still was unfathomable. Going to school was unattainable. I was chained to my home by the malevolent power in my brain that promised me the world was vicious. No one knows how any of it started, but I was sure that it was never going to end. The pain I had felt at eleven was incomparable. I was certain I was going to die. I spent afternoons in my bed screaming "GET IT OUT OF ME" and throwing up dry Cheerios that were too innocent to stay in my anxious stomach. I stopped feeling like a human being. My dog was afraid of me. And most obviously, I was aghast at what I had become.

It took immeasurable time to redevelop the human being I was . . . and to develop her even stronger.

Somehow, sleepless weeks turned into doing my homework outside on my backyard deck. The only thing that could slow me down was the nature of Nebraska, the chirp of blackbirds the second week of March. (And *Harry Potter*, but I'm trying to talk up our state here.) The sky was blue for a consecutive week. The clouds leapt out of the way so the sun could only shine on me. I could breathe. It was strained and painful and seemingly impossible, but I could breathe. I felt warm and capable—as capable as I could be. Slowly, I returned to school. I wrote about my illness for *Huff Post*. I sang my praises to the world outside my house.

If the world in which I had originally lived refused to be my home, I refused to accept the negativity. Nebraska wanted me to stay. Even though I didn't cheer on game day, Nebraska wanted me to win.

The trees in the woods behind my house were full of leaves one day and bare and snowy the next. The suburbs swallowed me whole, and I was finally thankful to live three streets away from school and from the people who encouraged me to show up. Hy-Vee beckoned with fresh fruit and guilty pleasure Chinese food. There was a Walgreens, a dentist, and a dry cleaner's on every other corner, and somehow, it was still hard to remember street names. It all felt like a small town, but if I drove far enough away, I could touch the seventh-floor newsroom of the *Omaha World-Herald*. Everything was in walking distance, but we all had cars. National news was hard to watch, but state competitions for journalism meant something to me. Nebraska became significant. Home became palpable.

Suddenly, in the way that people fall in love, children spill a bowl of cereal, or ironically enough, a panic attack hits, I realized that I didn't want to leave this one-horse town. I wanted to stay here, and I wanted to own the horse.

In my life, especially at this point, I don't think I would thrive so naturally anywhere other than the familiar blush of the Great Plains. I still love the ocean, mountains, and theme parks. I still love getting lost. But I don't want to live and dwell day to day in the territory of the untold and the unvisited. Those are special events, stories that I can only tell because I know what home looks like.

Here. Now. In the state that raised me to be the woman I am today. An imperfect, blossoming human who forgets to shave her legs, eats three Pop-Tarts some mornings for breakfast, and has been brought up to be fearless.

Nebraska, you are the backdrop of my biography. The good life that keeps getting better. Let's keep growing together, because I have a feeling that no matter where I go, we will be great friends.

You're the heart of the nation and the red in my veins. Thank you for building me up, humbling me, and being my muse. Keep in touch.

Becoming Vegan in Western Nebraska

LANE CHASEK

Panel-selected prize winner in nonfiction

Grandpa Jack killed a heifer with his bare hands when my dad was eight years old. My dad was climbing the windmill near the house when he looked down to see Grandpa Jack in the nearby pasture fixing a faulty water pump as a young heifer approached him from behind. Maybe it was the fact that he hadn't had enough coffee and was nervous that morning. Maybe the sound of the heifer's hooves plodding over the damp earth startled him. Or maybe he just sensed the heifer's presence and, not having time to think, assumed it was an intruder on his property. No matter what the cause was, my grandfather turned his entire five-foot-five, two-hundred-pound frame around and put all of his strength into punching the heifer's side as hard as he could. Something inside the heifer must have broken: either a rib came loose and punctured a lung or maybe a blood vessel in the cow's heart burst. The heifer tottered, fell to the ground, and jerked its hind legs a few times before finally dying.

My dad only told me this story once, which is odd. He has a habit of repeating stories, especially stories about people killing animals or animals killing people.

"That was the worst I've ever seen him," my dad said. "He just stood there, took off his hat, and stared at the heifer for a few minutes like he couldn't believe he had that kind of strength in him. That night my mom was making a tenderloin, but he refused to eat it. He said he just wanted potatoes."

For the next two weeks Grandpa Jack didn't eat meat. Grandma Betty made him nothing but potatoes because there was nothing else to eat in the house. Soon she started to worry about his health so she drove to Chadron and bought him some cans of fruit cocktail. Grandma Betty didn't think the human body could survive without animal protein so she put marshmallows in his fruit cocktail because, she reasoned, marshmallows contain gelatin. She honestly thought she was saving his life. But Grandpa Jack had never liked marshmallows. He didn't like the pale, soft grapes in the fruit cocktail, either. So after every meal he left behind a bowl of wet marshmallows and grapes.

But after a month he started eating meat again.

"One night I put a chicken breast in front of him," Grandma Betty told me. "He looked at it at first like he didn't know what it was. Then he cut a piece, put it in his mouth, and started chewing. From then on he just ate meat every day as if nothing had ever happened."

The summer before I went to college I helped my dad repair barbwire fences in Beaver Valley. The fences were there mostly for decoration and to indicate where property lines were. Not that property lines meant much anymore. Most of the families in the Valley had moved away at least twenty years ago. Our nearest neighbors, the Deadles, had all either died or changed their names by the time I was born in 1994. But my dad said it was important to remember who owned what, even if they were dead.

At one point we came across a small enclosure fenced off with seven strands of barbed wire. It was near a windowless, unpainted house that had become tilted by the wind.

My dad shook his head and spat into the enclosure.

"A hog pen," he said. "You can tell because it has seven layers of wire instead of the usual three to five." My dad shook his head some more, and I could tell he was clearly disgusted at the thought of hogs living in Beaver Valley.

My dad explained that hogs, unlike cattle, have no respect for fences or property lines. If they were fenced in by just three layers of barbed wire, they'd destroy it. So the only way to keep them in line, he explained, is to surround them with as much wire as possible, maybe even attach nails or razor blades to the wire just to be careful.

I couldn't imagine having to do this. I'd never raised pigs, never had to be near one, and the little I knew about them came from media such as *Babe* and George Orwell's *Animal Farm*.

My dad seemed to sense my doubt and said, "They're smart as hell, but when you feed them they don't see you as a person. They see you as a food source. So let's say some old woman or old man who lives alone trips and injures themselves while feeding their hogs. For a while those hogs won't know what to do. They have nobody to feed them and nothing to eat. And that old person, because they can't reach the phone, is just going to be stranded in the pen. So what do the hogs do? They eat their owner."

My dad and I spent the next five hours tearing down the hog pen and replacing it with something more modern and acceptable. The whole time, my dad told me the stories he'd read in newspapers about people being eaten alive by their own hogs.

He said it happened mostly in places like Wyoming, South Dakota, and North Dakota, places where old people often lived alone and neighbors were scarce. When neighbors or authorities eventually found their bodies, they were often missing their lips, noses, and ears. Sometimes the hogs even gnawed off their fingers.

"If they were decent animals," my dad said, "they'd just go for the throat and get it over with. But if they did that, they wouldn't get to see their captors suffer."

Grandma Betty refuses to believe that pigs could be that smart. She's told me this many times. For eighty years she's also believed that mountain lions were introduced to North America from Europe and that all male mountain lions died out in the 1950s. According to her, that's why mountain lions and other large predators in North America are becoming so rare.

Two years ago, when I still ate meat, I became obsessed with researching the Ossabaw hog. Originally from Spain, the Ossabaw was introduced to Spanish colonies in the Gulf of Mexico in the 1500s. This breed of hog eventually made its way to Ossabaw Island in present-day Georgia, from which the hog takes its name. On this island, the Ossabaw evolved to become smaller and, as an invasive species, began to outcompete and kill off most of the island's native fauna. Many of them became feral and hunted rats, reptiles, amphibians, dogs, and even deer. At one point the people of Ossabaw Island feared the Ossabaw hog was a threat to human life, so the island's local government began paying people to exterminate it.

Today the Ossabaw hog is smaller and tamer. It's an easy breed to identify. Its coat is thick and bristly, usually a patchwork of brown and black spots. As piglets, their coats are black and white, similar to a dalmatian's. While pork continues to become safer and blander with time, the Ossabaw's meat has become somewhat of a delicacy. Along with the other breeds of "wilder" domesticated hog, the Ossabaw is prized for how dark and marbled its flesh is.

I think this says something about the American diet: we still want to eat something wild and untamed. Even in an age in which the vast majority of us get all of our food from a grocery store, we still want to imagine we're eating something dangerous, maybe even forbidden. Even if it's bad for us, even if it's something only our distant ancestors had to eat or kill for survival, we'll still eat something as long as it resonates with some primal chord in us.

There are deep sociological and psychological reasons why stories

like *Oedipus Rex*, *Paradise Lost*, and even the book of Job have reso-
nance today. But I think the rules laid out in Leviticus speak to us
and tempt us in a way even Freud or Jung couldn't put into words.

I have a Turkish friend who, in his own words, "converted me to
veganism."

When I told my maternal grandparents in Rapid City about my
new lifestyle, they thought I was killing myself.

I wanted to tell them that eating meat was only going to kill them
quicker. I wanted to tell them that maybe all the pork and beef they
ate was the reason my maternal grandfather had heart palpitations
now. I wanted to tell them that meat was probably the reason he also
had to have two bypass surgeries in the past seven years. I wanted
to tell them about all the videos my Turkish friend had shown me,
videos of cows being forcefully inseminated so they would produce
milk and of chickens being electrocuted before being processed.
I wanted to tell them that saying there's such a thing as humane
slaughter is like saying there's such a thing as humane murder. I
wanted to tell them about all the studies I'd been shown by my
friend, the medical literature that had both edified and terrified
me for weeks on end, thinking about what I'd been doing to my
body for all those years.

But instead I told them not to worry. I promised to take care of
myself. To further set them at ease I even told them I'd take supple-
ments. Though I could have told them the truth, I knew conventions
and traditions, no matter how destructive they may be, can never be
destroyed by one person.

People have told me eating other animals is a part of human nature.
Animals eat other animals all the time, they argue. The problem
with this argument, I've realized, is that it's completely accurate. As
humans, we love to kill each other and ourselves, and I don't think
anything will change that. So I have no choice but to admit that my
meat-eating friends are right and I'm in the wrong. Even though I

like to think I'm acting morally, I'm still on the wrong side of history and evolution.

I once wondered what it would take for an herbivorous animal like a cow to become a carnivore.

In eighth grade I went camping with my brother on the outskirts of Crawford, Nebraska. The second day we were there it started to rain ceaselessly, and we ended up staying inside our tent, living on jerky and potato chips, for an entire day.

To pass the time, I read a book I'd brought with me by Edgar Rice Burroughs titled *Beyond the Farthest Star*. I remember this book so well because the copy I owned had a full-color ad for Newport cigarettes placed in the middle of it.

The story itself is underwhelming. An American man is shot in combat during World War I and miraculously finds himself transported to another planet where humans live in a semi-utopian republic that's like a cross between the Garden of Eden and Aldous Huxley's *Brave New World*. The people on this planet are mostly blond, blue-eyed, beautiful humans, and their government officials all take IQ tests before they're allowed to take office. There's also a war the American protagonist fights in, but by then I was already bored with the story.

It's been almost ten years since I read that book, but there's one small detail from it that I still remember vividly. In this world, horses and other equine species were used as livestock, while bovine species were ridden as horses and were often used to transport soldiers and weapons.

I tried to imagine what a fierce cow would look like if it wasn't a bull. I imagined Zeus just before he raped Europa, with crystal horns that spiraled into the air, maybe with crazed, bloodshot eyes and blood dripping from his mouth. But I don't think that's the image I'm looking for. No matter how hard I try, a cow's eyes will always be too soft and pleading, its eyelashes will always be too long for them to look vicious to me. So I could never imagine them eating meat.

Or maybe I just have a bad imagination. After all, I still can't picture horses or ponies being used as vehicles of war.

Sometimes I have a dream in which I'm finally married to my girl-friend and we're living together and raising the perfect Middle-American vegan family. The dream becomes a nightmare when we visit my family in western Nebraska and my parents, grandparents, aunts, uncles, and cousins are shocked and even horrified that we're not eating meat, eggs, or dairy. Some of my female cousins, who probably slaved for hours to cook for us, will be offended when we won't eat their meals for health and moral reasons. Most will just be confused. Some, like my cousin Bo in the army, will make jokes about low testosterone and the size of my penis.

Eventually my new family and I will have to eat like Grandpa Jack for that one month he didn't eat meat. In the nightmare, my family and I are forced to sit at a separate table with paper bowls of fruit cocktail and damp marshmallows in front of us. We eat our fruit cocktail silently, picking around the marshmallows and grapes.

If I were forced to construct a definition for "diet," I wouldn't be able to. I don't know what counts as food anymore. I don't know what we as humans are meant to eat or should eat. I don't think anybody truly knows, not in today's world in which factors such as socioeconomic status, religion, culture, geography, education, and science make it impossible to clearly define what's healthy or ethical in all situations. Sometimes I wish I could live in the times of the ancient Hebrews and read Leviticus like it was the Food Pyramid. Whether it comes from God or the FDA, we all crave guidance, something or someone to tell us right from wrong.

I don't know if I could tell the difference between herbivores, carnivores, or omnivores now, either.

Last summer, I was driving alone to Alliance, Nebraska, to visit my mother and her boyfriend. Along the way, I noticed something in a field to my right. A cow had just given birth, and her calf was sucking at her teats, its legs wobbling and its chin dripping with milk as it took part in this ancient mammalian tradition. The mother cow, meanwhile, was chewing on a gummy, bloody heap of her own placenta.

I pulled my car over to watch. I'd seen this same scene before: mother and baby, Virgin and Child, a scene so universal and integral to us as mammals that we've constructed entire religions around it. This should have been mundane to me, but for some reason I stopped to watch this time.

It was still early morning. The placenta in the mother's mouth was crusted in dry grass and mud, and it steamed in the cold air. After they give birth, it's not uncommon to find cows eating their placenta. Placenta is a natural cornucopia of nutrients, something that should never be wasted in a world where survival is never certain.

As she chewed, the mother didn't seem to notice the calf beneath her, didn't seem to realize that she'd just given life and was giving further life in the form of her milk. Instead, she kept chewing her placenta.

Just then I spotted a brown-and-white paint horse sneaking up to the cow and her calf, its head hung low and its hooves plodding heavily over the ground. It came face-to-face with the cow, took the other end of her placenta in its mouth, and started chewing on it. The cow must have noticed. Her eyes were open and she likely looked the horse in the eye, but instead of reacting in any way she let the horse have a share of what her body and nature had made for the both of them.

I sat on the hood of my car for nearly an hour. I didn't leave until the cow and horse had eaten the last of their meal, the sky a pale, glowing pink behind them.

Hatchet House

LUKE GILBERT

Those who enter the schoolhouse find out soon that they will never leave.
For the Hatchet House claims its students for eternity.
Be wary when near and never step inside.
The teacher is waiting to take your head and your precious life.

The air was cooling, and as summer drew to an end, autumn was beginning to set in. It was Friday afternoon in Papillion, Nebraska. School had just gotten out for the students of La Vista Junior High. For eighth graders Cale, Connor, and Tommy, this usually meant going home and playing hours of video games for two and a half days straight until Monday morning rolled around again. This weekend, however, was going to be a tad different. By nightfall the three were in Cale's basement hashing out the remaining details.

"Alright, my parents should be in bed and asleep around 1 a.m. We'll just hang out down here until then. Connor, you got the flashlight?"

"Yeah, I got it. Except I'm pretty sure these stupid batteries are going bad on this piece of crap." Connor proceeded to hit the side of the flashlight. It flickered for a moment then stayed on. He waved it around for a few seconds then switched it off.

"All right, I'll go check upstairs for some before we leave. Tom, you bring your sister's camera?" asked Cale.

Tommy let out a deep sigh. "Yeah, I got it, but dudes, I don't know about this. I'm starting to think it's a bad idea."

Connor interrupted, "Stop being such a baby, T. Nothing bad is going to happen. We are gonna go to the schoolhouse, take a picture of ourselves inside, and then leave. Simple as that. Jenny and Megan just did it last week and said it wasn't scary one bit. We will be fine."

"Yeah, but . . ."

"No buts. That jerk Ryan bet us sixty bucks we couldn't do it, and I'll be damned if we let him show us up."

"Connor is right, Tom. This won't even be that bad. It will take all of five minutes once we are there. We get in. Take the photo. We get out. You are just letting your emotions get the best of you."

Tommy indeed was letting his emotions get the best of him, but it wasn't like he was being that unreasonable. The destination where they were heading was not a nice place. Everyone knew that. It was called the Hatchet House, originally named the Portal Schoolhouse. It resided just south of Papillion in the small town of Portal. Why was Tommy so scared to go there? Well, the story went that many, many years ago a teacher went completely insane and one day locked all her students inside the school and beheaded each of them one by one. To that day people still thought the small building was haunted by the teacher.

"Yeah, but Jenny and Megan never took a photo . . ." Tommy quietly added.

Just then Cale's younger brother, who was sitting at the top of the steps, came down and peeked his head into the basement.

"Mark, get over here," ordered Cale.

Mark approached the three boys and said nothing. Mark was only seven years old. He was a pretty quiet kid, but he listened to and admired his older brother very much.

"What are you going to do if Mom and Dad come downstairs and we are not here?"

Mark answered as if he were practicing what he was going to say, "I'm going to text you and tell you they came downstairs."

"Good man." Cale smiled and handed Mark a one-dollar bill. Mark grabbed it and ran upstairs.

"Do we even know how to get to this place?" asked Tommy.

"Yeah, I overheard my sister talking about it with her friends the other day. We will just take our bikes down the Antelope Valley bike trail, and that should get us pretty close to the wooden bridge. Then we just go over that and follow that dirt road until we reach the school," said Connor.

"We are sure we won't get in trouble for like trespassing or anything like that?" Tommy asked.

Connor responded, "Tom, do you know what 'abandoned' means? It means no one is there. No one will be there anytime soon. We are not gonna get in trouble."

The boys waited around in the basement playing zombie games, eating junk food, and talking to pass the time, then 1 a.m. finally rolled around. The three of them put on a few layers each to stay warm.

"All right boys, we ready to go?" whispered Cale.

"Let's do this," replied Connor.

Tom said nothing.

The three climbed through a small window in the basement that opened to Cale's backyard. Mark watched from inside as his brother and two friends left into the night. The air was cool and crisp. There was virtually no wind, and the boys could see the condensation from their breathing.

Cale forgot to go upstairs to check for batteries.

"Follow me," said Connor.

The three boys biked through the seemingly deserted night streets until they reached the beginning of the Antelope Valley trail. The trail meandered through a dense forest of trees and bushes.

"All right, it should be about ten more minutes of riding, and then we should reach the bridge," declared Connor.

The street lights disappeared, and the darkness of the night consumed them as they rode. The boys stayed close to each other as they peddled deeper into the wooded trail. The only thing to light the way was Connor's janky flashlight, which seemed to flicker on and off every minute or so. Those ten minutes felt like two hours to Tommy. Each passing moment made him feel more and more on edge. The trail was dead quiet. No leaves rustled from the wind. No living thing made a sound. The silence was unnatural. The only thing the boys could hear was the crushing of dirt and gravel underneath their spinning tires. The boys finally reached the wooden bridge Connor had mentioned earlier. They could hear the small river's water flowing, which helped drown out the eerie silence. The bridge was about one hundred feet long and around seven feet wide. It didn't look "safe" to cross over by anything larger than a golf cart. There were no guardrails, and it looked as if it could collapse at any moment.

The air became thicker, and a slight breeze began to blow. Leaves blew by their feet.

Tommy spoke up, "Dudes, I think we should go back. I'll give Ryan the money and say it was my idea not to go to the schoolhouse. I'll say I chickened out."

Tommy could feel the sweat forming on the back of his neck. He clenched his sister's camera with both hands. The soft breeze cooled his perspiration, and a chilling wave came over him.

Connor glared at Tommy with a sinister grin on his face and said, "You know this bridge is actually called Heartbeat Bridge. Supposedly when that looney teacher killed all those kids she cut out their hearts and dumped them in this river. People say when you cross over the bridge, you can still hear the heart . . ."

"*Shut up, Connor!* You're not helping the situation at all!" barked Cale. His voice echoed through the night air.

Tom said nothing and just stood there. His body became very tense, and his eyes opened as wide as they could.

"Will you guys relax!? We are fine! I'm just messing with you a little bit. Come on, we are almost there," assured Connor.

Reluctantly, Cale and Tommy followed Connor over the bridge. It creaked and slightly shook. Every step Tommy took he felt more and more beside himself. He held the camera tightly as he peeked over the edge of the bridge to gaze at the murky black water. After they crossed the bridge Tommy noticed the breeze had picked up. It was now a mild wind that began to cut through the night air. It whistled by their ears. The darkness was all around them. The light from the flashlight appeared to be getting dimmer, but that might have just been Tommy's nerves acting up again. After about five more minutes of biking the boys reached the schoolhouse.

The wind came to an abrupt halt, and the dead silence came back. The air grew even thicker with each passing moment. The three dismounted their bikes and faced the small schoolhouse. It was quite run-down and battered. The wood siding was rotted through and hanging in various spots from the building. The once white paint had all but been stripped away by time. There was a large green door with two green glazed windows, one on each side. The door had a large crack down the center of it, and a hole remained where the handle used to be. On each side of the schoolhouse there were three windows about three feet apart from each other. Covering each were brown wooden shutters. Some had fallen from their mounts and collapsed to the earth, revealing the green glass caked with dirt and infested with cobwebs. From the outside, this place surely seemed abandoned.

Connor quietly spoke up, "Okay, let's do this. Remember we each have to take a picture of us sitting in one of the desks."

There was a strong gust of wind; Connor's flashlight flickered off and on again. Their bikes were knocked off their kickstands and fell to the ground.

Tommy's legs quivered beneath him, and his whole body began to tremble. "Dudes, I'm just gonna stay out here and wait for you . . . Two photos are enough to prove we were here."

Connor interjected, "Tom, you didn't come all this way to punk out and just wait outside. Now man up a little bit, and let's get this over with."

"You'll be fine, T. Remember, in and out," assured Cale.

Tommy looked at both his friends and grudgingly agreed, "Okay, fine."

The three began to walk toward the large green door in a single line. Connor led the way with his trusty flashlight. Cale followed in the middle, and Tommy trailed behind the two. Tommy could feel his heart, every quickened beat pounding inside his chest. Cale's palms began to perspire. Everything was silent except for the ground beneath their shoes as they took each disturbing step. Connor approached the green door and rested his left hand on it. He gently pushed it open. It groaned softly. The boys could see nothing inside the schoolhouse except utter blackness. One entered after the other. Silence engulfed them as they carefully took each step. Tommy left the green door open behind him as he fully entered the dark void. All three were now inside the schoolhouse.

The boys followed the dim light from Connor's flashlight as he scanned the room. At the back stood a teacher's desk; in three rows stood the students' desks. Each row had five desks, one following the next all the way back toward where the three boys stood. There were fifteen in total. Despite the dilapidated look from the outside, the inside of the schoolhouse seemed to be in decent condition as it appeared to the boys in the thick darkness. The desks were in perfect straight lines, and the wood flooring looked well maintained. The walls were clean and had been painted white. Connor slowly walked toward the front where the teacher's desk was positioned. Cale and Tommy stayed still, Tommy still clenching his camera, Cale beginning to feel quite uneasy. Connor approached the teacher's desk. As he scanned the top with his flashlight, a small tattered piece of paper caught his eye.

Connor spoke. "Look at this, guys."

Cale and Tommy approached the teacher's desk slowly and stood next to Connor. Connor reached for the paper, shined his flashlight (which flickered once again) on it, and read aloud:

Those who enter the schoolhouse find out soon that they will never leave.
For the Hatchet House claims its students for eternity.
Be wary when near and never step inside.
The teacher is waiting to take your head and your precious life.

A large gust of wind came, but not from the entrance where the green door stood open. It came from the wall behind the teacher's desk. The burst of air slammed the green door shut. BANG! The boys looked up from the paper and directed their eyes toward the green door. The flashlight flickered again.

"Ahhh!" shouted Tommy. His camera fell to the ground. He bent over, grabbed it quickly, and stood back up. "Dudes, let's go!" He was shaking all over.

"Tom, it was the wind!" shouted Connor. "You are freaking out about nothing."

Tommy made his way to the green door and put his hand through the hole where the handle used to be. He tried to pull, but the door would not budge.

"Guys, the door won't open!" He yanked at it as hard as he could. The green door did not move. "Guys!!" Tommy implored.

Cale scurried to the green door. "Watch out, Tom!" He nudged Tommy aside and placed his hands inside the hole. Cale pulled with all his might. The door refused to move. "Connor, the damn door won't open, man!" Fear flowed through his voice.

Connor looked up from the paper. "You guys are freaking wimps. How hard is it to open a door!?" He put the sheet of paper back on the teacher's desk and began to walk over to the other two boys and the green door. Without warning, the flashlight went out. The darkness engulfed the schoolhouse. The boys were blinded by the blackness.

"Connor! Stop fooling around, dude!" shouted Cale.

"I'm not fooling around!" He hit the flashlight with his hand and clicked the switch from on to off repeatedly. Nothing happened. "It won't freaking turn on, guys!"

It was hard to actually tell if Connor was telling the truth. On one hand he was known for messing with the other two quite often, but on the other, there was a distinct quavering in his voice.

Tom shouted, "I can't see anything!" He clenched the camera as hard as he could. His heart raced. His skin tingled all over. His eyes frantically searched the darkness for any point of reference, but he couldn't see a single thing. Cale opened his phone to use the screen as a light, but it did not come on.

"Guys, my phone is dead for some reason!" Cale said. He smacked it a couple of times, but nothing happened. *"Come on!"* He smacked it again—still nothing.

Connor shouted, *"Ahh!"* There was a loud crash of one of the desks. The sound alone was enough to make Cale and Tommy lose any sense of composure they may have been holding onto.

"Connor!" squealed Cale. "Connor! Where are you?! Holy shit! Connor! Connor!" Connor did not respond. "Please, man! Stop messing around! This isn't funny anymore!"

Another loud crash, and a second desk fell to the floor. A loud scream came from Cale's voice. "Cale! Connor!" Tommy shouted. "Guys! Where are you?! Please, guys! This isn't funny!" He could see nothing but the blackness. His breathing increased. He aimed his camera out in front of him, turned the flash on, and snapped a photo. The flash created a brief moment of light. All Tommy could see in that minor moment of sight were four desks: the two that had fallen over, one that still stood, and the teacher's desk at the front of the room. Nothing else was in the schoolhouse.

His heart felt as if it were about to explode. His whole body shook as his spine tightened. The floor convulsed beneath him. Without warning, something knocked Tommy to the floor. *"Ahhh!"* he screamed. His camera flew from his hands and skidded across the wooden floor. As he lay on the ground, growing more frightened and hopeless, the room grew bitingly cold, and the perverted air penetrated Tommy's entire body. The darkness. The silence. Pure terror. It was all Tommy knew at that point. He stayed lying down and began to whimper. An unknown force grabbed hold of Tommy and lifted him into the air. Tommy screamed at the top of his lungs, "*Ahhh!!*" as he was dangled above the floorboards of the schoolhouse. The force thrust Tommy into the desk that still stood. He could not move any part of his body. He screamed as loud as he could. He was completely paralyzed. He screamed for his life. The camera flashed three more times, but Tommy could see nothing at this point. Tommy let out one last shriek, then something firm hit him in the head, and he was knocked unconscious . . .

The morning came. Back at Cale's house, Cale's parents, worried sick, had discovered the boys had left the house and were calling everyone they knew to try and figure out where the boys had disappeared to. Mark disclosed to his parents that he had overheard the boys talking about a schoolhouse. Cale's parents reported what Mark had told them to the police. The police officer, Officer Gilbert, figured that the schoolhouse they mentioned was the one in Portal.

"Kids will go there late at night to mess around. A lot of the time they will sleep there and what not. I wouldn't worry, folks. They are probably there right now. Should be waking up soon," Officer Gilbert assured the alarmed parents. However, the officer wasn't exactly sure. In fact, he had never been to the schoolhouse in Portal, nor was the info about other kids going and spending the night there factual. He did truly believe the boys were fine and simply just wanted to calm the parents down. "I'll go check it out for you and get back to you with what I find."

The officer took his motorcycle out to the schoolhouse in Portal. He crossed Heartbeat Bridge and arrived at the schoolhouse shortly after. The air was silent. He dismounted his bike and approached the green door. He pushed it open. He kept the door ajar. Inside he saw nothing but the teacher's desk and the fifteen other desks, set out perfectly in their three rows. The sky became abnormally dark, almost sunless. The burly clouds shrouded the schoolhouse in an ominous shadow. The officer walked slowly up to the teacher's desk. On the desk lay a photo and a tattered piece of paper. The photo was facing down. Gilbert grabbed the worn piece of paper and read the words written on it to himself.

Those who enter the schoolhouse find out soon that they will never leave.
For the Hatchet House claims its students for eternity.
Be wary when near and never step inside.
The teacher is waiting to take your head and your precious life.

He smiled ever so softly and let out a short chuckle under his breath. He placed the piece of paper back on the teacher's desk and went to grab the photo. He flipped the photo over and revealed what the camera had captured just hours before his visit. His face froze, and his eyes filled with complete horror.

Displayed in the photo were three desks. On each desk, placed perfectly in the middle, were the heads of Connor, Cale, and Tommy. The officer's face went pale as death. His skin became ice cold. He dropped the photo back onto the teacher's desk and stumbled backward. Just then a gust of wind came from inside the schoolhouse. He turned and faced the entrance to the schoolhouse and began to sprint toward the door. His attempt was in vain. The green door slammed shut.

My Dad Is Dead

AMANDA HOVSETH

"Amanda . . ." My brother's voice breaks, like he's choking on something. "Amanda, wake up."

"What? Yeah, Giles, what . . ." I'm answering before my eyes open, my mind determined to respond before my body is willing.

"Dad's dead."

"Wow, really?" Wow? Did I really say "wow"? How did Giles get in here anyway? The door is open . . . I left the door open. When I went to bed a couple of hours ago I felt like I needed to. Twenty-six years old and still superstitious—ridiculous. Good. It would have hurt him to have come down to a locked door.

"Yeah." He coughs. "It just happened . . . just now."

"Okay, I'm coming." I reach for my glasses. Can't wait for contacts, in a hurry . . . a hurry, why? Time is already up. Dead. Gone. Permanent. I put on my glasses. My brother has left already; he's waking up our other brother, right outside my room. My baby brother, the youngest, my babyest. Dad's dead. My room is dark, but light shines through the opened doorway. I hurry toward it.

I am twenty-five years old, back in college, and looking forward to a road trip home with my dad for Thanksgiving break. When he says he is proud of me now, it feels real because I am finally proud of myself. I had never really believed him before because a silent voice inside had always read the undertones in his words as disappointment. But now my first book is published, and the majority of reviews are positive—his review is positive. He stops at every bookstore, school, and church on his road trips to tell them of my book. His ceaseless peddling of my work has shown me he believes I have something worth saying.

He's temporarily stationed in Arkansas for the railroad and is going to drive out of his way to pick me up. We will have seven hours alone together, and I am excited to talk to him about my new life, my new future.

My phone rings; he tells me he is running late. He took a nap after work and ended up sleeping much longer than anticipated. I say it's okay because I'll just nap while I wait for him.

Five minutes later he calls again. He sounds tired, and he stumbles over his words. His boss said he has to work later that day. I might as well drive myself, and we will meet back home. He is very sorry. We hang up, and I stare at the phone. It's okay. I will still get to see him at home. But a realization penetrates my hopes: he has never missed family time for work before. He has always talked his way out of or into anything he wants. He is a real-life con-artist. It doesn't compute. I shake my head and smile. He's an easily distracted guy; I'm sure it's nothing.

I use the bathroom and then grab my bag to leave. My phone rings. It's my mom, probably to check on our travel status. I answer. There're two seconds of silence . . . "Mom?" She sobs. I put my bags down. "What's wrong?"

"Have you left yet?"

"No, just about to."

"Good, you might need to go to Arkansas. Your father had a stroke; he's in the hospital. He says he's fine, but I know he's not. I'm sorry, you're the closest . . . he needs someone there."

"Okay . . ." I check Google Maps. "I can be there in eight hours." She thanks me. "I'll head out now." We hang up.

My phone rings. "Mandy?" My dad's voice is soft and wavers as if he is half-asleep.

"I know, Dad, Mom just called me. I'm on my way to your hospital." I prepare for an argument. For him to say he's fine and my mom shouldn't have imposed . . .

"Are you sure?"

"Yes, I want to come."

"I'll text you my room number when they tell me."

"Love you, Dad, see you soon."

"Love you too."

I'm eighteen years old. My dad's calling me a stupid bitch and shoving me backward. I fall onto the couch. My mother screams. *"Don't you ever! Don't you ever talk to my daughter like that!"* She runs at him and is pounding his chest and arms with her fists. He tries to block her blows while moving her away. She stops, exhausted, and drops down next to me, pulling me into her arms. My dad is pressing his palms to his forehead. He throws a chair across the room. Then he grabs car keys and heads out the front door. My mom is telling me not to listen to him. I barely hear her. I've never been called a bitch before, probably never will be again . . . at least not by someone who knows me.

I'm twenty-three years old, in a hotel in San Antonio. It's just me and my dad; he's been stationed here by the railroad, "borrowed out" they call it. He didn't want to go alone, so I decided to come at the last minute. We've been here a month and a half now. He walks into the hotel room. I sit up in bed.

"Dad? You're back already? How'd you get back?" Normally I have to pick him up from the depot when his trains come in.

He's ruffling his hair, and his eyes look hollow. He sits down to undo his work boots, but I can tell his skin is crawling. I wait. He'll talk—it's usually hard to stop him from talking.

"I hit a guy with my train. A boy. A man. He was in his twenties." He glances at me every once in awhile as he talks but never makes eye contact. "He just stepped out in front of the train. I think he had headphones on. They phoned his parents . . . came to the tracks . . . apparently his brain wasn't right . . . he was . . . autistic or something."

"What? Why was he walking alone if he was autistic?"

"I know, right!" My dad is looking in the freezer, probably for ice cream. He pulls it out and puts it back; his skin is pale. "Some people just don't . . . they just don't think . . . I've hit cows before. Those trains they really leave nothing. Just pulp, barely tell it's human. He wasn't even close to the size of a cow." He's opening a bag of beef jerky.

"You know it's not your fault, right? You can't stop those trains in time. If you could have, you would have."

"Of course it's not my fault!" He paces back and forth across the length of the room. "No, I'm okay. I could see him there from a ways away. He was just walking, and I thought he would stop. I honked the horn just in case. He just kept walking. I thought for sure he would stop, why wouldn't he stop? Everyone stops. Then he didn't . . . he just didn't . . . stepped right out in front. Train didn't even bump. We pulled the brakes. I thought maybe he'd made it across, where I couldn't see. Trains take a long time to stop though."

"Are you fired?"

"I thought for sure I would be, but no. They want me to see a therapist, and I have three days off of work. I told them I don't need a therapist, it wasn't my fault, I had no hand in it. His parents didn't even think so. Said he was living on his own for a year now. His roommate didn't know he was autistic." He takes a bite of his jerky. "Did you have plans for today?"

I do. I had planned on meeting up with another railroader's wife and daughter and going to see the Madame Tussauds Wax Museum and Ripley's Believe It or Not. I ask if he wants to join.

He wrinkles his nose. "No. Call me when you're done though."

"I can stay if you want."

"No, no, Mandy, really I'm fine. It wasn't my fault." He's pacing again.

"Of course it wasn't, but we can go another day, when you're at work."

"Really," he raises his voice and waves me off. "I'm fine. Call me after."

I leave the room and go to the museums. My phone is turned off inside because it's proper etiquette, but when I make it to the gift shop and turn it on to call my father, I realize I have six missed calls from him. My stomach flips, and I call him back.

"Hello?" he answers, and the phone crackles from wind blowing past. "Mandy? Where've you been?"

"In the museums. I just got done and called you."

"It took that long?"

"Yeah, I guess."

"Well, I'm out front."

I turn to my friends and tell them where I'm going. As I walk to the front of the museum I spot him on a bench. He smiles and waves, but his eyes still look hollow. My heart aches. Poor guy, I should have never left him alone.

I'm nine years old, and I've had a sleepless night. My parents are up, yelling at each other. I am lying in bed, pretending to be asleep and wondering if my sister in the bunk below me is actually asleep or if she is crying silently as well. I think that perhaps I should climb into bed with her and comfort her, but I don't know how. And if she is asleep then I'd only wake her up. So we lie alone.

It's the next morning. I slip into the bathroom to use the toilet. My mom is in the shower, but there is only one bathroom so we often double up.

She steps out as I'm brushing my teeth, and I notice a long, dark bruise on her right thigh. I ask if she's okay. She insists she is, that she doesn't even know how she got that bruise.

My dad is nowhere to be seen. Someone has obviously tidied up the living room. Part of me is worried my dad won't come back. The other part knows that when I return from school there will be a new vase of flowers in the window, and my parents will be waiting to hear how my day went. Like every time before.

I'm twenty-six years old. I've come home for the summer because my dad has been diagnosed with cancer. Turns out he never had a stroke, only seizures brought on by brain tumors. My parents found me a job in road construction. I work anywhere from eight to fifteen hours a day. I'm walking up the stairs at five a.m. to get ready for work. My dad is awake in the living room. He always wakes up to send my brother and me off to work. He is looking at his phone. The low morning light allows the glow from his phone to accentuate his bone structure—sharp edges that used to be concealed in muscle. I wonder at how quickly his athletic physique has abandoned him.

"Mandy! Good morning! Have you seen these pictures of Giles and Jamus?"

Jamus is one of my cousins; he's four years old and can't digest any food at all, so he lives solely on a powdery nutrient substance. Quite frankly if people didn't know he was sick, they wouldn't guess it. He has curly red hair and chubby cheeks that even cherubs would envy. He enjoys labeling days as "Hug Day" and then distributing hugs throughout the house. When he has an allergic episode he dresses up as Iron Man and faces the situation head on. He is just absolutely adorable and ceaselessly cheerful. He also loves my father, calls him his best friend.

"Yeah." I chuckle. "Jamus is super cute."

"I know!" My dad lets out what is best described as a girlish squeal. "I just keep thinking he couldn't be any cuter, and then I flip to the next picture, and he is still even cuter!"

I laugh as I scoot my mom's cat out of the way and head out the front door.

His voice trails after, "I love you, Mandy, and I'm proud of you."

He has said that every morning this summer.

I don't know who makes it to the stairs first, me or my brothers. It doesn't matter—we are all walking through the kitchen. My mom is on the phone.

I'm twelve years old. My dad is standing by the stove with a big butcher knife in his hand. Neighborhood kids are watching and gasping as he continuously flips the knife into the air and catches it while making various faces of fear and shock. Tootsie Roll, our little Yorkshire terrier, is hanging out by his feet. I call her over and pick her up. My dad glances my way, and I frown at him. He knows this type of thing worries me. He calls out, "What, Mandy? You don't trust me?" Then he throws the knife even higher. I roll my eyes and leave the room. He can insist on dropping a knife on his foot, but he can't make me watch.

I am nineteen years old, and I don't know how many days I have been lying in bed. I share a house with two friends. My dad hadn't wanted me to move out. He yelled and yelled, calling me a fool for wasting the money. Then he scoured my new apartment from top to bottom, looking for ways to make it safer. I don't know what I am doing with my life. College is boring, and the end seems so far away. I haven't picked a career and have no idea how to go about doing so. And I just keep gaining weight no matter how much I work out. A month ago this doctor gave me antidepressants, and I don't know if I've left my bed since. I've missed every single college class, and I'll tell you what, I couldn't care less. I couldn't care if the world caught fire and burned up right in front of me. I couldn't care if a masked man entered my room and skinned a box of puppies. I couldn't care if Orlando Bloom asked me to dinner.

My phone rings. I answer. It's my father. I can barely hear him. I'm not sure if he's on speakerphone or if I'm still half-asleep. While he talks I stare at the wall that I painted pink five months ago. The call is short. He tells me he loves me no matter what. He knows I'm going through some stuff, and I might be worried he'd be disappointed. But he's not, it doesn't matter, he loves me anyway. The phone is beeping now. He must have hung up. I pull it away from my ear and notice the time. It's time to take my antidepressant. I pick up the box and roll onto my back. I hold the little white pods in front of my face and stare at them. The sun sets outside my window, slowly obscuring my view. I blink, throw the pods at the trash can, and stand up. It's time to take a shower.

I'm two years old, it's the middle of the night, and my mom is pulling me out of bed and bundling me into the car. I ask her where we are going.

"To pick up your father."

It feels like we have driven forever. I am lying with my head resting by her pregnant belly when we pull up in front of a bar. I know it's a bar because of the neon lights. All bars have lights like that. She tells me to wait in the car and grabs a bat from the back seat. I wonder if my dad needs it to loan to a friend. Then she pauses and puts the bat back down.

Minutes later she is stomping out of the bar with my dad stumbling behind her, a bright red imprint of a palm on his cheek. They both get into the car without saying a word. I climb onto my dad's lap, and I sleep the rest of the way home.

I turn the corner into the hallway. I know he will be there, at the end and to the right. I know he will. But he won't. I don't want to go. I have to go.

I'm twenty-four years old and at a Friday night Bible study with my father. People are asking him about his testimony. I smile because I know my dad doesn't like giving his testimony. He says that everyone thinks their life story is worth telling, and most people are wrong. They insist. So he gives them a piece of information that I always suspected but never confirmed until then.

"When my lady told me she was pregnant with Mandy I panicked. I knew I should marry her and take care of the kid, but how was I supposed to do that? I was just a kid . . . I gambled a lot then, had gotten in too deep with the mafia. I started watching Oprah at my mom's house, thought it might help. It didn't much. My brother . . . the one, he's in Omaha now but was in Alliance, Denny, his wife got me an interview with Union Pacific Railroad. So I drove through the night, from Chicago to western Nebraska, took the test, and they gave me the job. I figured the mafia goons wouldn't drive to Nebraska lookin' for me, 'cause really, you can't squeeze a dry sponge anyway. It worked. I paid them off later . . . But if it wasn't for Lori's pregnancy I would have never looked to leave. If I had never moved to Nebraska I would have never met Pastor Rich. And if I had never met Rich, I . . . who knows for sure, but I think I would not have ever been convinced of my need for a Savior. I thought I was good enough to make God happy. I suppose everyone thinks that. Ironic isn't it, wanting to earn love and failing when all along I could've gotten it for free?"

I'm twenty-three years old. I just graduated from Bible College. My dad has called a family meeting. He wants to study the book of Proverbs. It's a good idea in theory, but family meetings never end well. This time it's my fault.

I'm mad. My stomach is clenching, and my jaw is tightening. He's picked a study guide that is full of big words and nonsense phrases and ideas. I try to explain, "Proverbs is simple. This book is ridiculous. Man's way of overcomplicating God's Word to make ourselves seem more sophisticated." Normally my dad would understand this. I know for a fact he would agree with that general statement. But this isn't normally, this is a family meeting, and something goes wrong.

I'm grabbing my backpack, mentally calculating what is inside—my wallet, laptop, flash drive (with all my stories on it), phone—while I'm yelling at my dad and telling him I'd be better off alone. He yells back, something like, "Go ahead then!" I slam the door and stomp two miles to the library.

It's been five hours in the library. I have friends I can call, plenty of friends who would let me move in as long as I need. Even a couple of guys I know who would welcome the chance to get closer to me, guys my dad wouldn't approve of. But if I called them, if I called any of them, then the world would know. The world would hear of times he yelled, the time he broke our kitchen table, and they would see nothing else. They wouldn't actually see him and how much he truly has changed throughout the years. Everything he has worked for, everything I have worked for, would be ruined.

I'm walking through my parents' front door. The rest of my family is in the living room, quietly reading various books and watching TV. They look up when I come in, nod, and keep reading. My dad isn't there. I wonder if I can sneak into my room and pretend like nothing happened. Our cat, Shale, is walking by. He pauses in front of me. Shale was a rescue, so he's always hiding, never making a peep. Normally he runs when the front door is opened; instead he looks at me and walks down the hallway. I follow him. He leads me into my parents' room. My dad is on the bed with his back toward me and a phone in his hand. Shale jumps up onto the bed and meows. My dad turns around.

Instantly I start crying. And I say, "It's not worth it. I came back for the people we love."

My dad is on his feet and hugging me. "I'm glad you came home. I didn't know where to look."

I'm twenty years old, and I work as a secretary at Regional West Medical Center. My main job is organizing patients' charts and putting doctors' orders into the computer. It's been a hard twelve-hour shift, and I'm exhausted when I walk through my parents' front door. A couple of my friends are over, so I try to put on a smile. My dad isn't fooled and instantly notices my sour mood. He insists on knowing what has upset me. I keep it simple because I want to move on, telling him the job is hard because I seldom get bathroom breaks and the doctors are pretty rude. He's furious. He calls my friend

Andy over, grabs a phonebook and the car keys, and asks me what the doctors' names are. I ask why he needs their names. He says, "No one gets to be rude to my daughter, no matter who they are!" Despite his rage, I smile. He and Andy plan on teaching the doctors "a lesson." I know what type of lessons my dad teaches people, and I know our town needs its doctors, no matter how rude they are. So I convince him the doctors weren't rude to me specifically. They are just rude in general, and it annoys me. I really am okay. At this point I'm beaming at how protective my father and friends are, so he believes me and is content. Instead of teaching lessons, he and Andy make homemade Chicago-style pizza.

I'm five years old. We are driving across the country, back home from my grandmother's funeral. It's nighttime. My parents laid down all of the seats in the back of our red minivan so that we have a huge bed. I stare at the stars through the window and listen to the consistent calm of the wind blowing past. My grandmother is dead. I cried when they told me, even though I barely knew her. I knew the concept of a grandmother, and mine was dead. Then I saw her body. It was white and cold, painted and posed. It was not her. They placed her body there, but she was not in it. I crawl to the front of the van and sit, leaning forward between my parents' seats. I want to know where Grandma is.

They tell me they are not sure. But then they tell me something my father had just learned himself but that my mother had known since she was young. Grandma could be in Heaven if she had trusted God to get her there. They just don't know if she did.

I feel chills. How does someone trust God to get them to Heaven?

They tell me that every time we do the opposite of what God wants us to do, we have to be punished for it. If we decide to try to handle the punishment ourselves, then He can't let us go to Heaven because that's the punishment. But even when God is angry, He loves us and wants us to go to Heaven. So He decided to take the punishment, Himself. He came to Earth as Jesus, never did anything wrong, and then was killed in our place. Now we have a choice: we can pay for our sins ourselves, or we can believe that Jesus already paid for them and accept that payment as a free gift.

I tell them I want Jesus to pay for my sins. They teach me how to pray. That night I meet God. I have never felt more like I could fly than at that moment. I breathe deep. I tell my sister about it, and she joins me in prayer. Then I go to sleep, trusting my dad would get us home safely and knowing my God would someday bring our souls home safely.

I step into my parents' bedroom. It smells like a hospital: disgustingly sterile. My dad's body is there. His eyes are open. One is staring in a different direction than the other. His mouth is also wide open. It has been that way for days; he slept with it open. My mom has turned off the oxygen machine and taken the tubes out; he doesn't need them anymore. Its constant clicking and blowing was a reminder of how much it hurt him to breathe . . . but now the world sounds wrong. We all step in, take a look, and leave. My mom is calling my uncles. They will be over soon. She says she has already called hospice. I say I am going downstairs to change since company will be coming.

I hurry back up the stairs. One of my brothers is telling the other that he needs to touch my father in order to make it real. The other is protesting, saying he doesn't need to. I brush by quickly and say, "Don't push him into anything. We all grieve different." Then I'm back in my parents' room, alone with my father. I step up to him and place three fingers under his jawbone as if to take a pulse . . . I'm six years old, and I've had a nightmare. I know if I wake my father up he will let me climb into bed and I'll be safe. I can sleep easy . . . No. No. I'm twenty-six years old. I'm touching his neck. His skin isn't quite cold yet. He's not waking up. He's not moving. He's dead. My dad is dead.

I say, "I love you, Dad. I'll see you later."

I'm twenty-five years old, it's Thanksgiving break, and I've made it to the hospital in Arkansas. My dad is in the hospital bed. He's on the phone with our pastor. I hear him struggle to speak, so I step into the bathroom to give him privacy. It's on speakerphone, so I can still hear. My dad is always worried cell phones will give us cancer, so he doesn't like holding them up to his head. Our pastor doesn't want to let my dad give up hope. He says, "There's still a chance. You could survive . . . you're not dying before me." I stare at the sink because I don't want to look in the mirror. My dad says, "No, listen. You know the story of John Bradford, right? I want my kids to know. I want, after all this, the one thing they should learn from my life . . . 'There, but for the grace of God, go I.'"

I take my fingers off of my dad's neck. I walk out of his bedroom and into the bathroom. I close the door, and I cry.

Living Statues on Highway 77
Spectators of Nebraska
Memory Keepers of Waverly

SARA MOSIER

Living Statues on Highway 77

There is a curious smattering of headstones
In shapes
of dreams
of once-upon-a-time homes
that dresses the green and gold flesh of the Great Plains.
We don't expect you to recognize us, tucked away along
    Highway 77,
beneath
endlessly open skies that showcase stars like dust left behind
  from visiting gods,
    while our feet are still settled in the cornstalk-ridden soil,
      waiting for the eyes of the sun to wear us down
        slowly,
    but surely.

Our bodies are naked of color,
     the days before the vanity of paint, we represented stability
       in a vast and empty landscape.
   We'll swallow up the sounds of the meadowlark song,
     The soft hum of cicadas in neighboring trees reminding us
We still exist.
We're still here.

Spectators of Nebraska

    All-knowing gazes that peer out onto the plains
broken window-pane eyes
   their sight may be shaken,
the flesh of their bodies dressed in bright green vines that trail
   from basement to attic
that wither and fall
to snow that mimics endless jars of spilt glitter
they stand stubbornly behind trees
gnarled by the greedy breaths
of dancing Twisters,
those unpredictable creatures
that take ownership of their place on these open lands,
and yet they stand,
a murmur,
a whisper from the past.

Memory Keepers of Waverly

We hold hearts that
    Have long since stopped beating,
spent voices that trickled down the staircase,
withering and settling into the cracks of the
    weather
        worn
            floors
and we catch them all, the laughter, the promises, the cries
we gather them close in our palms and as our shells dissolve,
    we encompass the souls
into the
    damp
        hungry
soil.
    You left us behind
to defend ourselves
    misplaced sprigs of wheat donned our porches.
our only defense
    against the greedy and tumultuous
screams of the North winds
against dampening snow that swallows up
    our collective voice,
    gusts that ruffle the shorn golden stalks next door
an acid cold that will slowly shed our skin
    our insides peeling, and tearing away
no feet to grace our floors,
    no voices to fill our halls,
no warm breath to squelch our
    loneliness

there is a saddening solace in our
    destruction
We have become our own graveyard,
    A crumbling tombstone,
    A beacon of the past
And a reminder
    Of a simpler time

Road to Redemption

BRIANA DAVIS

As I ran, the trail blurred by beneath the soles of my feet. The path ahead was neither straight nor as twisted as the roads that wind through the mountains, weaving through the paths cleared of trees like slithering snakes of rock, tar, or cement. It was so narrow in places that I could not have run along the path with another person beside me, but it was as wide as my five-foot-five frame is tall in others. Smooth cement slabs only composed a very small portion of the trail, and there were not more than three or four slabs in a row without cracks along the edges. These cracks varied in size, some so small I don't even think I could have squeezed a dime into them. Others were large enough that if their depth had measured more than two inches I think that a walnut could have dropped through and become lost in the void. As if the unevenness of the cemented portion did not make it difficult enough to run on without twisting an ankle or tripping, patches of the trail were a mixture of dirt and sharp pink rocks about the size of golf balls. It seemed as though the cracks and uneven parts of this path that I was following were just waiting to make me stumble and even fall and scrape my knees and palms. The more closely

I scrutinized the route I had chosen to take on this run, the more I began to realize that it bore an uncanny resemblance to life.

My life has had a few curves, some of which have even thrown me for a loop as if I were back on one of the rollercoasters at Silver Dollar City in Branson, Missouri, for which I harbor resentment and fear. The simple, straight path represented my childhood, which as a young girl growing up in a traditional, Sunday school family seemed like it could not have been more picture perfect if it had been one of the beautiful stained glass windows of our church with the bright morning sun shining through. It wasn't until my own path diverged from the one that my family was traveling that I began to see through the façade of a life that I had lived for so long. I was a person with two separate identities that only intermixed if it was required to maintain my good-girl reputation. Both of which were so well played out that if I was fully immersed in the identity required at the time, no one could have thought that I could possibly have been an intruder. But my charade could only go on for so long.

As in many situations, my intentions had started off well. Ever since I had begun running with my brother on Sunday afternoons when the weather was nice, I had wanted to run on my high school cross country team. Running made me feel like I had talent—it made me exceptional, or at least that was what I told myself. In reality, I wasn't that fast. I didn't have strong legs or a good running form. Athleticism didn't run in my family; I was the only one who had even really wanted to participate in sports. Looking back, I can see now that it was my determination to go against the normal achievements of my older siblings. Not only did I want to excel academically, I wanted my name to be remembered. After all, the only people who remembered how smart you were in high school were your aging teachers, who had a tendency to retire within a few years of teaching our class in our small-town K–12 school. So one day at the beginning of August 2010, I made a choice: I was going to get in shape. My definition of "in shape" was probably not far off from that of the millions of people around the world who make a New Year's resolution to lose weight or work out more. The difference between the New Year's commits and myself was that I took it seriously, a little too seriously.

Since running cross country required logging quite a few miles, I determined that I would begin my journey where the soles of my feet could wage a war of speed and endurance with the paved, pink-rock-covered country road on which I lived. I started off well, and within a week of beginning my "Become the Fit, Strong, and Pretty Girl Everyone Is Jealous Of" training, I felt more energetic. So I figured I would take it up a notch; I would start watching what I ate. Junk food wasn't good for me anyway. All of those useless carbs and calories that my mom always joked would last a moment on the lips but forever on the hips had no place in my body anymore. I had never been picked on by other kids for being chubby or overweight, though I distinctly remember that my dad made a remark when I was in the second grade about how I could probably pinch more than an inch of my tummy fat. That was when I was still growing, and he was completely joking, as if he could be one to chastise anyone about having a little belly flab. As a constantly working farmer, he would go through at least a half dozen cookies, half a family-sized bag of Lay's potato chips, and handfuls of heavily salted peanuts on an average day.

My daily eating restrictions started out simple without any major cutbacks or restrictions, or so I liked to tell myself. I would eat whatever my parents made for breakfast, usually French toast or pancakes, try to not think too hard about whatever questionably edible objects I shoveled into my mouth at the school lunch table, and then sit down and dine with my family for supper. Eliminated from my diet were the midafternoon snacks that were a consistent staple of my life since kindergarten after coming home from a long day at school. I replaced them with doing all of the chores required to feed the cattle on our farm followed by at least a three-mile run. *It wouldn't be this way if they had just let me join the cross country team this year*, I told myself. Within a week of cutting out snacks and whatever foodstuffs I viewed as nonessential, I determined that simply cutting out snacks wasn't enough. I still wasn't feeling like I was in good running shape and thought that it was due to my caloric intake. Portion sizes began to decrease, and soon I found myself consuming only one plain pancake for breakfast, claiming that I didn't have time for any more or even to put syrup on it.

"Hey!" Mom said one morning as I grabbed a pancake and a water bottle before rushing to tie my shoes. "Come back here! You have to have more than that for breakfast! You won't be able to focus in class!"

"Don't have time!" I shouted back as I shut the door behind me and began walking down the gravel driveway to where the school bus would be waiting in less than a minute.

When I ate school lunches, which were meager to begin with, I became like a bird pecking at seeds and only devouring a very small portion. Evening meals did not change much, though I replaced the usual glass of 1 percent milk with a glass of water instead. To administer any drastic change to my eating habits at the supper table would have incurred rounds of questioning that I had no desire to endure.

People at school began to notice my slimming figure. Girls in the grades closest to me would say how jealous they were that I was so skinny. Their praise washed over me like refreshing rain, encouraging me to push the limits even more. All the while I justified the running, completing all of the chores single-handedly, and eating restrictions by telling myself that I was just trying to look like those girls you see on the covers of magazines who have the slim and toned bodies. I was secretly envious of them, but unlike other teenage girls, I didn't want to be skinny, I wanted to be "fit." I made sure that I told myself with an air of superiority that I wasn't one of the girls struggling with these things called eating disorders.

Late in September, I was leaning over beside a friend and showing him how to do something on one of the school computers when he looked up at me and asked, "Are you anorexic?" Immediately, I became defensive and denied it, responding by asking if he was crazy. Prior to that day, I had never even entertained the idea that I could be a victim of such a thing. A thing that would take a stick of dynamite to my self-worth and reduce it to nothing more than ashes scattered across the road on which I ran every single day.

I realized that somewhere in the midst of that path that looked so smooth and straight I had stumbled and fallen. My knees looked as if someone had taken a cheese grater and scraped it on my skin over and over until they were raw and bloody. Little stones had lodged themselves in the callused skin of my palms, making them sting. As I struggled to stand upon my own two feet, I cringed in pain and squeezed my eyes shut to try and stop the tears. Resisting was futile, however, and I knew that once the first few droplets were released, the torrents would not be contained again. How had I come to this point? What had caused me to fall? I didn't understand where I had first begun to stumble and lose my way because my mistakes were often masked by good intentions and vain choices that I made to try to somehow hide or dim the pain of my failures.

I was adamant that I was not the one girl out of every one hundred aged ten to twenty who is the unknowingly willing victim of such a thing as an eating disorder, as the Anorexia Nervosa and Related Eating Disorders website states. Although I am sure that my parents noticed my increasingly thin arms and legs and my collarbone protruding even more awkwardly than normal, they didn't say anything. They were preoccupied trying to find an effective way to treat my dad's anxiety, which seemed to dampen his energy irregularly like clouds coming and going on a partly cloudy day. Around the middle of October, I actually began to weigh myself on the old, oval-shaped brown scale with a little dial on the top and duct tape holding it together hidden in the back of our bathroom closet. I was around 105 pounds at that time. A week and a half later I weighed 103, and soon the practice of setting foot on that piece of metal and plastic that I allowed to determine my self-worth became a pre-shower ritual every weekday morning.

As I struggled to my feet I saw a mirage appear to my right through my tear-filled eyes. I blinked, and the figure came into focus. It was a girl. She had perfect form, slender and toned legs, long brown hair, and a pretty face. Ponytail bouncing as she quickly jogged across the street toward the path on which I stood, she looked like everything that I had strived for. Everything I wanted to be. Pretty. Athletic. Skinny. Smart. She took off down the path from which I had just come, and without hesitation I turned around and began to follow. At first the steps hurt, but soon the pain became a dull ache, easily ignored as my feet pounded harder and harder against the ground.

I told myself I wouldn't drop below 100. That was my limit, my "ideal weight." For a five-foot-five-and-a-half girl who had started off around 112 pounds, I deemed it a reasonable and healthy goal. I began to view my desire to become the "fit girl" like many of the New Year's Day dieters do, strictly based on what the scale says. One day toward the end of November, I woke up and walked down the hallway to the bathroom to shower, quietly opened the closet door to pull out my trusty scale, and stepped on it. The little dial read "98." *I am doing better than I thought!* I told myself with a sense of foolish pride and satisfaction. *Pshhh! Skip only going down to 100. I'm going for 96!* Why 96 pounds instead of 95, I do not know. But it was as if that one little extra miniscule line on the scale dial would save me from having to consider that something was seriously wrong.

After coming home from school one day, I walked into the kitchen to get a drink of water from the refrigerator and noticed a 9x13 pan of freshly baked apple crisp sitting on the top of the stove. The smell of the apples tossed in cinnamon sugar, then sprinkled with a streusel mixture and baked to perfection at 350 degrees gripped my senses; I ate about a fifth of the pan within ten minutes. Setting the fork down on the table, I realized how awful I felt. The apple crisp that had tasted so good in my mouth began to settle like a rock at the bottom of my shrinking stomach. Pushing the pan away I quickly ran outside to do the chores so that I could go on a longer run. There was no way that I was going to let all of that sugary goodness ruin my goals. Following the run I felt as if I was going to throw up, not because I was sick but because the thought of forking any more food into my mouth that night made me nauseous. My mom had supper waiting. It was one of my favorite meals, chicken and penne noodles with alfredo sauce, but

I refused to consume anything placed on the table aside from water and the fresh fruit salad.

"Do you feel sick?" she asked.

No, I thought.

"Yeah, I just don't feel very good," I replied. "I think I am going to go to bed early tonight so I'm not sick when basketball practice starts next week." She didn't ask any more questions, just told me that I at least had to eat some veggies in addition to the fruit, and then she left me to myself.

I watched the girl as I ran and sped up, trying to keep up with her. She kept eluding me, however. Always staying just out of my reach. I could feel the swish of the wind blowing off of her long ponytail, but I could never stretch out my fingertips far enough to touch or grab ahold of her. I pushed myself, trying to draw even with her, but she just kept increasing her pace. It was a constant battle to achieve something that I could not: perfection. I considered giving up. But I knew that if I quit I would have nothing to show for my efforts but a broken life. So I continued to relentlessly chase after this image of myself created to make me desire more. Continued to long for something I could never reach but chased nevertheless.

Basketball practice started the Monday before Thanksgiving, and I was thankful because the start of the sports season meant that I didn't have to try and get my run in before it got dark outside. I was even more grateful that we were required to have practice two out of the four days that we had off of school for Thanksgiving break; that way I didn't have to worry too much about overeating and then having every calorie add another fraction of a pound to the number on the scale. By the first of December, I consistently weighed in at 96 to 97 pounds. I was content with that. I would look in the mirror and be able to see the definition of what I told myself were my abdominal muscles, but it was really just my skin clinging to what little muscle tone I hadn't lost. My ribs didn't protrude very much, but if I had to do sit-ups in PE class I could feel most of the vertebrae that composed my spine rub uncomfortably against the hardwood gym flooring.

If we had to run a lot in basketball practice because of missed free throws, I noticed that I felt fatigued, and my world would spin for a few moments after crossing the baseline following yet another round of sprints. I associated the tiredness with a lack of sleep (I had never been a heavy sleeper) and the dizziness to the natural exhaustion that accompanies it in combination with dehydration.

The first two basketball games went fine, aside from the fact that our team lost. During the third game, right before our two-week-long Christmas break, my classmate and teammate's mother happened to sit by my mom on the bleachers. "Briana looks like she is all skin and bones out there. There is no way she can tough it out with any of those big girls. I'm kind of worried about her," she told my mom as they watched my 96-pound body attempt to play effective defense on a girl who had at least fifty pounds on me. "She has always been skinny," my mom replied. She knew that something was up, but I hadn't said anything, so she didn't think much about it. After all, I did come across as a pretty confident teenager, and deep down inside I think she was holding on to the hope that all mothers have that their daughters will share every triumph and difficulty with them. As my mom watched me play that game, she realized just how fragile I looked. So breakable that if one of the big five-foot-eleven girls fell on top of me, I would probably snap in two.

My mom was unusually quiet for the first few minutes of our drive home after the game. Then she told me about her conversation during the game.

"I'm worried about you too. You can't be doing this. It isn't normal. Honey, if you continue to lose weight you could die." I watched, silent, from the passenger's seat as her eyes began to glaze over. "That's almost what happened to one of my friends in high school, and eventually it did kill her. And I don't want that to happen to you. You need to start eating more."

"There's nothing wrong with me. I'm perfectly fine. I eat enough. See?" I grabbed the bag of puffcorn that she had bought to snack on while she drove for work and began shoving some into my mouth.

"No, you need something that has more nutritional value than that. At the moment, though, if you have to eat ice cream to not be completely skin and bones then that's what you have to do."

"Fine. I'll have ice cream when we get home." I pretended to stare out the window at the darkness angrily. *Yessss! Ice cream! An excuse!* I hadn't eaten ice cream since the summer and secretly was happy that my mom had said something about my weight so that I had a reason to allow myself to indulge.

A week later I wasn't quite as happy. Mom had taken it a little too seriously; she now said that if I wasn't weighing at least 98 pounds by the end of Christmas break that she was not only going to force me to quit playing basketball but would also take me to the doctor. Needless to say, I made weight only because basketball was pretty much my social life, but she still forced me to go see our childhood pediatrician. He didn't seem very worried about me. My bone structure was naturally smaller than that of my siblings, and my weight-to-height ratio for my age was not that far from the average. It wasn't until they received the results of the blood tests a week later that the phone rang with the doctor's voice on the other end of the line, sounding concerned. My blood sugar levels were extremely low, and other vital nutrients were as well. Before hanging up the phone, the doctor gave my mom the number of a psychologist who specialized in helping girls overcome eating disorders. Then the threats began.

"If you don't weigh over 100 pounds by January 10, then you won't be able to continue playing basketball."

And the next week was the same sort of thing except that the weight expectation increased by about two pounds. The only reasons I kept meeting the demands of my parents were because I turned the little knob on the scale so that it read about two pounds higher than was accurate (I convinced them that the little red needle never landed on zero because of how ancient the thing was) and because there was no way that I was going to have to tell my coach that I was no longer able to play basketball because I "didn't eat enough" according to my parents. By the end of February I weighed

105 pounds according to my deceiving scale. But my parents still weren't happy.

"If you don't start making an effort on your own to gain more weight back, we are going to set up an appointment with that counselor."

They left the piece of paper with her name and phone number sitting out on the counter as a reminder of the threat. *What the heck,* I thought. *Obviously I had to make an effort on my own to get this far. It's not like they were holding me down and forcing me to chew and swallow.* My parents didn't see my effort; they only saw that I wasn't where they thought I should be at that point. So the counselor was called just after basketball season ended and an appointment made. Both of my parents went with me for the first session. I told them it was a waste of money. That it wasn't going to help at all or change anything. The counselor's office was located in an expensive office space in the middle of a neighborhood where you could see swimming pools and full-size basketball courts over the tall wooden fences.

During the second session the counselor got right down to business. She wanted me to keep a notebook, more like a diary, of the foods I ate throughout the day over the next two weeks. I told myself I didn't have time to keep track and would sometimes purposefully and accidently forget to write down meals. The third session I "forgot" the diary in my locker at school. When I finally brought my notebook back and gave it to her during the fourth session a week later, she looked at it briefly, flipping through the half-empty pages, and said, "Why didn't you write everything down? We can't get anywhere if you aren't willing to do what I ask." *Ha!* I thought, laughing to myself. *I don't have a problem, so I don't know what kind of "progress" she thinks she is going to make.* After looking at my food diary, she told me to go sit in the waiting room and send in my mom to talk. Later my mom told me that the counselor had sat her down and bluntly asked, "So did you not notice anything wrong with Briana's eating habits? Why didn't you take action sooner? This could have been prevented with a little intervention."

I'm sure her heart was in the right place, but after the fifth counseling session (or as I fondly thought of them, "I have a PhD but I am going to make you and your mom feel incompetent" sessions), we simply stopped going. The only rewarding thing I got out of those hours of skipped classes in the afternoons was cutting my long hair off and donating it to an organization that would make it into a wig for another person. Somehow those foot-long strands of hair going to someone who needed them to feel pretty again helped me more than the hundreds of dollars' worth of counseling. You can't change someone who doesn't want to admit that a change is needed.

Soon I realized that my efforts were futile. But I didn't want to admit it. She knew she had me following her as intently and trustingly as a duckling trailing its mother across a busy street to reach the peaceful pond on the other side. Except unlike the cartoons, I didn't have a policeman with his whistle to stop the traffic and keep me from getting hit by the ignorant drivers of attacks on my self-worth that hit me like speeding cars. Fully knowing that I was captivated, the girl turned off the path I knew, onto a new one. Glancing behind her, she looked to see if I would follow or turn away.

My freshman year of high school ended without much excitement. I was still very conscious about not gaining "too much weight" but had begun to be a little smarter about it. Summer relieved my pressure to fit in, and with people no longer staring at me all day, I didn't worry as much about how flat my stomach was or what I was eating. Those three months of break I discovered that when I dropped as much weight as I did, I wasn't losing just the stuff under my skin thought to be fat—I lost muscle too. I felt an exhausting weakness, almost as if I were about to faint at times after running. As the summer went on and I gained back some of the muscle I had lost during my attempts to find my self-worth, I began to feel stronger.

As an incentive, my parents let me go out for cross country during my sophomore year, and I loved it. Running just to run was always more enjoyable for me than competing, but I would take a grass path over running in circles on a tarmac track any day. That first year of cross country I missed qualifying for the state meet by one place. Only the top twenty runners had the privilege to compete on the big stage, and I came in twenty-first. I became determined to qualify for state during my junior year and trained hard over the summer. I still watched my weight and what I ate, to an extent. If I believed that I had eaten too much, I would go on a longer run than normal or add in an abdominal workout for the day. Ironically, those workouts that I sometimes thought would make me feel content with my calorie consumption for the day actually made the number rise on the scale. At first I wasn't happy about that, but then someone told me that muscle mass weighs more than fat, and I couldn't deny the strength that I now felt when running.

My junior year I qualified for the state meet by placing twelfth out of about fifty runners. I almost cried as I crossed the finish line at regionals, fully knowing that I had accomplished more than I had ever expected to.

I watched the girl I had chased relentlessly for so long jog a ways. Finally I tore my eyes from her image for the first time in my life and walked away. I began to run on the other path at the fork in the road. And as I passed the intersection of her path and mine, I felt that piece of me that had been chasing her for so long fall away. Like little pieces of shattered glass. It had not left me unscarred. She had chosen her path, one of brokenness and regret, and I mine, one leading to joy and redemption.

Cottonwood

CATHERINE PEDIGO

Panel-selected prize winner in fiction

For a small midwestern town of five hundred people, Milton had a tremendous cemetery. The gate was old, rusted wrought iron that creaked on its hinges a little bit with every passing breeze. There was an old, tarnished bronze padlock that held the gate doors together and had for nearly twenty years. For most of those twenty years, the gate had remained locked except for funerals. Now the groundskeeper had quietly told the pastor of the church that he would be leaving the gate open daily and would begin closing it again once the mourning had had a long chance to grieve. The lock hung resolutely from the gate, watching silently the haunts and their long, black coats that passed by it nearly every hour.

The quiet office of the pastor was oppressive, with windows opened wide for the hope of a breeze, but only the humid heat of an oncoming summer storm leaked in, like tar. The pastor looked out his window to the cemetery—the view was too clear; he could even read the nearest tombstones with their older dates, lined in neat rows that dissolved into a haphazard mess with the progressing years—to see the latest burial. The coffin didn't look very expensive, with dull wood that smelled still of sawdust. It was new, as was the flag draped possessively over it.

There was a large family gathered around the coffin, with three younger children being reined in by their siblings. Their mother, her weathered face wet and shining, pressed her lips together to sew in the sobs while the bishop spoke. The pastor had been unwilling to share the cemetery with the Irish-Catholics initially, but he had broken down after the third widow entreated him for the space. Their cemetery had always been too small and was now filled.

The boy had two brothers and three sisters; two of the girls were still dressed in crisply starched nurse's uniforms. Their eyes were weighed down, nearly closed, with lost sleep. They would undoubtedly return to the hospital after the funeral. Omaha had boasted about Milton's hospital because it catered to the larger Nebraska area; now, wounded soldiers were being shipped in by the dozen. Of course, there were rumors that larger hospitals had even more problems. Supposedly in even the best hospitals, soldiers were still forced to sit three to a cot in the hallway while they were examined. There weren't enough beds anywhere in the country to hold the sick, wounded, and dying.

A rare breeze ruffled the skirts of the women as they were leaving the cemetery, rustling through the low-hanging branches of a cottonwood tree that hadn't seen much water that year. The mother and her children passed by another woman, dressed in resolute black. The single mourner passed by the family like a shadow, no one whispering a polite "hello." The feeling of death was too heavy on them all to remember niceties.

The groundskeeper was limping to find the boys whose job it was to fill the graves. When he reached the mourner he paused, and her steps slowed as well.

"Big storm coming," he said, making a gesture toward the sky. "Best get home when the sky turns yellow." She nodded.

He had seen her before and knew that the grave she sought was on the left edge of the cemetery, the tombstone still a shiny marble, covered with the pollen and leaves of the cottonwood above it. It was a nice grave, perfect for the woman buried in it, who'd been a bit of a belle of the town before her untimely death. She'd been a nurse at the hospital, and one of the boys she'd tended had brought back some sort of infection in his blood. She and another nurse had died.

The mourner held out for the groundskeeper a folded bag with a large, wet stain that had seeped out with the heat that escaped the enclosed pastry. He thanked her, and she smiled blandly, leaving him to his work. The grave was as it had been the previous afternoon; the swirls of fingertips left in the coat of pollen were intact. The mourner wondered if the incoming rain would wash the pattern away or cement it in the clumps of sticky yellow powder. There was a patch of worried grass to the side of the stone where she had sat a few days ago, staring at the stone as if waiting for it to speak and pulling blade by blade out for an hour.

The mourner moved around to the back of the stone, resting her elbows in the pollen, not caring that the sleeves of her coat would be stained a greenish-yellow. The cemetery was nestled on the hill that overlooked Milton's main stretch. The hospital was directly below, a building that breathed death and illness. Even though she was too far to smell the rotting, medicinal smell of medicated bodies slowly decaying, she knew the odor. The bakery she worked in was across from the hospital. There was a constant circle of nurses there, sipping their burned coffee and whispering softly about their patients. If the mourner tried very hard, she could almost see *her* nurse there too, leaning away from her companions and against the counter to chat. There was always a free biscuit for her, but nowadays nobody stayed to chat anymore.

The clerk of the general store across the street from the hospital was a pleasant, wrinkled old man with a sympathetic smile. When haggard soldiers with grim stains of unease under their eyes passed through, asking for the "Cottonwood Cemetery," he would smile, nod, and point them up the hill. Cottonwood Cemetery wasn't an official name but one derived from the sheltered tunnel of cottonwoods that stretched their boughs over the stone and earth in the long, narrow cemetery to give the dead a little shade from the hot sun of Nebraska's summer. A beaten path wound its way down from the mouth of the cemetery, along the side of the hospital road and to the main stretch of Milton. It wasn't hard for a strange man or two to find his way once he knew where to start.

There were three soldiers standing at the entrance of the cemetery, looking through the gate doors that rose up like bent and jagged teeth in the mouth of a tobacco chewer. Though they wore no uniforms, their posture—straight back, clenched jaw, eyes fixed on the horizon instead of the stones lined in front of them—gave them away. One wore the sleeve of his jacket pinned inward, a cloth substitute for the price he had paid to fight in a war. The one in the middle was dust covered from head to toe, except for the jarring glimpse of white gauze underneath the collar of his shirt. The third held a crutch by his side, arm wrapped around the top as if hugging an old friend.

Finally, the one on the crutch moved forward a step, then another, hobbling into the cemetery. It was nearly empty, except for the groundskeeper plotting the space for a new grave and a mourner standing in front of a tombstone. The soldier knew who he was looking for but didn't know where to start. The back of the cemetery was organized in neat, straight lines. The front was overcrowded and haphazard.

"His name, son?" the groundskeeper asked quietly over the grinding and cracking of joints as he stood from his kneeling position.

"Baker. Neal Baker."

"Four from the big cottonwood." The soldier almost asked which cottonwood, because all of the trees in the cemetery were cottonwoods, but he quickly figured out which one the "big cottonwood" was. It was clearly the only tree that hadn't been planted intentionally, and the rusted fence of the cemetery sprouted from each side of its round and leaning trunk before weaving behind the row of cottonwoods planted to either side of it. Its branches drooped with the weight of its years, skimming the fingers of the smallest twigs over the tops of the stones close to its perimeter.

There was a single, jagged row of headstones jutting out from the farthest front edge of the trunk, since the boughs were too close to the ground in the back half of the tree. He counted from the tree to the fourth stone, three down from where the mourner stood. Struggling over the grass with his crutch, he stopped in front of the stone, steeled himself, and looked. It wasn't a good inscription. It just had his name and a note that he had died in the Milton Medical Center.

Neal had no family. The soldier had promised to visit him in the hospital when the stretcher had taken him away. He'd never had a chance before the memo came back with a list of soldiers who'd died in Milton. The bullet had broken through the soldier's ankle the day after, and he had woken up in a fever in Milesville, with the St. Agnes nuns. He remembered clutching a nurse's wrist and begging to go to Milton, to be buried there. He thought someone had agreed to obey his wishes, but he could not remember.

There was nothing to be said to the cold, rough stone with its heartless words. The soldier could not promise that somebody would remember him as more than a bleak headstone, and he could not promise that the war would end.

"Your sweetheart?" the soldier asked suddenly of the mourner, letting his eyes slip to the much nicer stone she stood before. He couldn't read the writing—he was too far away—so he glanced at her face and saw a ghost of a smile pass through her eyes.

"Yes," she said, her voice unexpectedly gummy and rough for someone who looked like a breeze would blow right through her. "Yours?" she asked, nodding toward Neal's stone.

"Friend. Had no family."

"And everyone needs someone to cry over their grave."

Self-conscious, the soldier adjusted his grip on his crutch to wipe at the grime on his face, but it was dry. Carefully, he navigated away from

Neal's stone and toward the mourner. The rows of fresh-cut stone were uneven and difficult for a man on a crutch. "What's his name?" she asked, nodding toward the soldier's abandoned post. He stopped. The mourner was standing in his sight line, and if she was just a foot farther from the grave, he'd be able to read her sweetheart's name.

"Neal." This time she did smile, her bloodless lips curling up like a poorly drawn moon.

"I'll keep him in my prayers." The soldier struggled for a moment to respond, but before he could speak again, the mourner nodded to him and swept past him, the flap of her coat brushing his knee. There was a whiff of violets and a hint of copper, and the soldier thought he might gag when the scent clogged his throat. Swallowing roughly, he read the name on the mourner's tombstone.

Though he was sure that she wouldn't hear him, he said aloud, "I'll keep her in my prayers." He stared a second more, committing *Nurse Margaret Fisher* to his mind, before he turned and walked the maze of the graves, his knuckles white with the effort of heaving himself through on his bad leg. The pain had flared up again, and he wondered if the hospital would give him a painkiller. Or just cut the damn thing off.

The mourner was only able to grieve properly on the hill of the cemetery. The bakery required that she wear a crisply starched white shirt and a brown skirt. Her black coat had to be hung on a peg in the storage room, and her handkerchief was tucked into her shoe. Customers didn't like it when she coughed in front of them, so she coughed underneath the counter, feigning that she was just grinding the beans. It was obvious, but people could still pretend to ignore her. The baker was leaving and reminded her to put on an apron before pulling open the back door and putting on his hat.

"When the sky gets to yellowin' just close on down and head home," he told her, squinting up at the suspicious gray sky. "This one won' be pretty."

"Yes, sir," she promised before the door shut. When she reached the front, the nurses were bouncing on the balls of their feet, trying to keep their heads from drooping like wilted magnolias. She heard the chorus of "coffee, coffee" and began to pour out the cups from a pot of coffee that was too hot and smelled sickly. Usually there was an undercurrent of talk, a discussion of patients and doctors and low supplies. Today there was silence, wide eyes, and a constant tapping of blunt heels to the concrete floor. The nurses were like gazelles, ears perked at the first sounds of a predator and waiting for the signal to flee. The storm was going to be a bad one.

Each shift of nurses was given fifteen minutes for a break, just long enough to march into the bakery and ask for coffee. The first quarter of every other hour saw the only customers, and the rest of that time was for inventory, sweeping, making more coffee, and silence. And when all of that was over, she leaned against the counter and stared out the dusty, smudged window toward the hospital. She watched as the soldier from the cemetery reached the end of the path and turned toward the entrance to the hospital, nodding his head and saying something to the person who opened the door for him.

A murky shape appeared in front of the door, blocking her view, and a person entered, surprising as that was. It was a withered old woman, with more wrinkles than skin and hectic light-gray eyes. Her hair was patchy and curled out of her head in brittle white spokes. Her head shook with the effort of staying up, and she shuffled forward, looking around in a daze. "Mrs. Kent," the mourner said softly, moving around the counter and holding out a hand, approaching the old woman like she would a stray dog.

"Charlie isn't at home," the woman said in a high, quivering voice that pierced the sound of coffee dripping. "Charlie. Where is my son? He likes his biscuits. Where is my son?"

"Mrs. Kent," the mourner repeated softly, her hand folding against the woman's coat. It had once been nice, fur, but had grown worried and faded. The creature it had been was dying once again. "Mrs. Kent, Charlie's up the hill. Charlie's been up the hill for a while now."

"He went out for a biscuit. Heard around town the draft was coming and wanted a biscuit. Have you seen him? Where is my son?" The mourner pressed her lips together tightly.

"I haven't seen your son, Mrs. Kent."

"I thought he might have gone for a biscuit. He likes his biscuits." The woman shook her head from side to side, realizing for the first time that there was nobody in the bakery.

"I'll give you a biscuit for him, Mrs. Kent," the mourner said softly, taking a biscuit from the warm tray on the counter and wrapping it up in a napkin. The old woman took the napkin-wrapped biscuit in a quivering hand before shuffling back out of the bakery. The mourner followed her to the door and held it open, looking up at the sky to watch its color change.

At five o'clock that afternoon, the mayor sighed and got up from the desk, hitching his suspenders up his shoulders, adjusting his suit jacket next. He could see the leaking yellow stretching across the sky and knew it was time. With a wistful glance and a growl from his stomach, he turned away from the barbecue shack he could see through his office window—they were putting out their closed sign anyway—and headed out. His secretary was already gone, and the single stretch that led from the audience hall to his office was empty of even echoes. His footsteps were muted against the tile floor and the wooden porch outside the building.

The street traffic had ceased, so the mayor strode right across the newly graveled road and up to the side entrance of the hospital, the one for the administrators. Keeping business away from, well, business. The head of the hospital was already standing in the lobby, arms crossed and white coat yellow in the reflection of the sky he studied through the window. "Time to close down?" he asked the mayor.

"I think so. Everyone's gettin' uneasy."

"I've had three doctors ask to go home early." The mayor ran his tongue over the fronts of his bottom teeth, wishing he had chewing tobacco.

"You know what to do then." The head of the hospital—a retired doctor who thought he was the most educated man in town—nodded and said nothing else. He didn't wish the mayor luck with the incoming storm, and he didn't ask if he could pitch in with the town's preparations. He turned, and he started talking to the nurse staffing the table. So the mayor hitched up his suspenders underneath his jacket and turned to leave.

"Mrs. Kent was wandering around out there." The mayor turned to look at the nurse, who'd stood up and was looking past the head of the hospital. "Bad time for her to be wandering. Might lead others to do the same."

"I'll take care of it," the mayor promised, tipping his hat before stepping outside. The humidity slammed into his nostrils; he breathed through his mouth, looking up at the sky again. It was almost entirely yellow now, only a few clouds left to be consumed. The mayor watched as the mourner who staffed the bakery, always wearing a somber look and a black coat, boarded up the front door and headed up the hill. His wife had said yesterday that one day she might just stay on the hill, and they'd find her there, next to Maggie's grave.

The mayor avoided the mourner's eyes, searching instead for Mrs. Kent. He had to walk down the street some ways before he found her huddled underneath a leafless tree, clutching a half-eaten biscuit to her chest. "Charlie?" she asked, her eyes wavering over the mayor's face.

"Now, Mrs. Kent, you know Charlie ain't down here. He's up the hill."

"Where's my son?"

"Mrs. Kent, I'll take you to your son," the mayor said, sighing and holding out his arm. The old woman's expression changed to one of abject joy, and she clutched at the mayor's elbow, thanking him and telling him how much her son loved biscuits. He had to walk slowly up the path, since Mrs. Kent could only shuffle, and he glanced up every few moments to check the sky.

The pastor emerged, silent as a ghost, from his church and met the mayor toward the back of the cemetery, next to a pollen-coated tombstone that read *Charlie Kent, Taken by the War but not from our Hearts.* "Mrs. Kent," the pastor said softly, nodding to the mayor that he could leave. The mayor eased Mrs. Kent's hand out of the crook of his elbow and placed it in the fine layer of yellow dust, leaving her with the pastor and her son. The mourner was standing at the entrance of the cemetery with the groundskeeper, who leaned against the gate waiting to close it. The mayor joined them, standing between the two and watching the pastor speak in quiet tones to Mrs. Kent. The sun was slowly sinking behind the trees on the hill, casting shadowed beams of light through the graves. They lit upon two more forms, solemn among the crooked rows from recent years.

Both were soldiers, standing in the cemetery solemnly as if they had no idea what they were doing there. One was missing an arm. The mayor didn't often like to think about the horrors of war. He was too old to fight a war and had no sons to fight a war. The war that had stolen away Charlie Kent and Maggie Fisher and others seemed distant, and he hated the constant reminders that the hospital thrived on. "I wonder whom they'll join," the mourner said softly, and the mayor looked down at her. She was nestled into her thick black coat but still looked cold to the bone.

"You'll see her soon, dear," the mayor said softly, answering the unasked question. The mourner smiled blandly before lifting her handkerchief to her mouth and coughing. The sound ripped through the silence of the cemetery, even attracting the pastor's attention as he calmed Mrs. Kent. The old woman was thrown across her son's tombstone, sobbing, even as the pastor pointed to her own. The pastor glanced at the sky once, then said something softly to Mrs. Kent. She seemed not to notice. He moved away from her, joining the mayor, the mourner, and the groundskeeper.

"It's time," the pastor told the groundskeeper, who hurried to shut the moaning gate of the cemetery in front of the three bystanders. "Their souls will soon be at rest." When the gate was shut, the groundskeeper moved away, and the mayor could see the shimmering outlines of other soldiers among the graves. They were less distinct than the two he'd already seen, having been restless in the cemetery for a longer period. The storm would take them all the same. The mayor looked at the mourner and put a hand to her elbow.

"Dear, I'll walk you home. Make sure you get back safely." When the last storm had gone through, taking Maggie's soul with it, the police had to drag the mourner away from the cemetery. She'd screamed all the way down the hill, blood and tears dripping down her chin and Margaret's ghostly imprint on the earth fading away with the wind.

Some Autumn Holiday

When It Happens

The Main Street Fair

DANIEL MCILHON

Panel-selected prize winner in poetry

Some Autumn Holiday

I suppose I should have been back there,
cozying in the maple shade
on my sister's patio
with my sweater around my knees
and ashy sausages gushing
their oily musk as they fizzled over the fire pit.
Perhaps I should have been with them,
the new in-laws,
graying the air with our breath and smoking mugs,
passing bowls of kraut between our pink fingers
and popping hot morsels like alms
into the collie's mouth when

it appeared with an expectant grin
between our legs.

That's where I should have been, I guess.

Instead, in a fit of whimsy,
I'd gone to the playground—
nothing more than a steel carousel
and an arthritic swing set—
rusting at the end of a dirt path
that ran like a dry brushstroke through
the amber maple litter and paper grasses,
far into the clacking trees and
around the scarlet bluffs
that cheekboned the neighborhood.

We'd found it that morning, my father and I,
on a walk we'd taken with my nephews
to break in their new sneakers.
They were the flashy sort,
chromatic explosions of
lacquered plastic
and cartoon faces
and blue lights that dazzled
with each leaf-flinging step
like some garish sea creature's
courtship display.

It was these lights that came to mind
as I toed myself
in creaking circles on the swings
and spied a spatter of blue jays
rising from the tree line,

flashing with each wing beat and
freckling the shards of marble sky
between the branches.

Eyes on the birds,
I rose and neared the screen of naked elms
and saw a bluff cut sharply downward
just beyond their knobby picket.
The plummeting earth opened
on a mousy pelt of bare woodland,
browed with an ocher horizon
of dry corn and
stark where dead trees shined
like white hairs in its aging scalp.

As the jays dove,
intent on the southern sky,
and flickered across
the static tree tops,
sudden phantoms
of roasted meat
and hearth smoke
possessed my breaths
and beckoned me
homeward.

I took a ginger step
backward, then another,
lingering,
still watching the blue fliers
define their glittering progress
before turning
to the path

and rasping on
cloaked ankles through
the auburn chaff
back to where,
I suppose,
I should have been.

When It Happens

When it happens
it can happen at the water,
I'd prefer,
where the willows dip their braids
and bare roots suture the riverside,
where sucking mud sheaths hooves
and stones wary soft paws,
where only dark beetles and silver flies
will come to nibble at my softness.

It can happen,
when it happens,
while the currents
dance my limbs,
as they dither
and cool
and my legs mix silt
into the mossy broth of their shallows,
as the willows spill like trickles of sugar
into the river's moony shellac,
as starlight tinsels the reed grass and pales me.

I'll deepen my breaths.

I'll ebb down the bank,
as gray waves dollop
gobs of mud over my bones
and sporous fibers hurry
my sustenance earthward.

Yes, when it happens
it will happen on its own,
I must insist,
with a throb,
fell thrum,
or roving misstep of the heart.

And as I go
some pious twist of breeze will catch
my final exhalation,
will rise
and join it to the wind.

The Main Street Fair

Driftwood and duck feathers
floated like tea leaves
in the night-stained water
as the lakeside carnival surged vermillion.

Fiberglass stalls wreathed in white bulbs
lettered their sizzling wares
through nebulas of steam and tobacco smoke
while children shrieked
from beaming carts and the whirring arms
of kaleidoscope gyros.

Heaping dunes of sawdust,
palominoed with clotting spills
and nomadic with scrawny gulls,
swathed the cobbled walkways,
and forests of sandaled feet.

I sat on the dock, cocooned in a sweater
on the sopping wood,
toes dangling like bait,
ears full of tidal sloshing
while the Ferris wheel made its signature rotations
just yards behind me,
its whirling spectra a galaxy on the black water
where red antennae and dimming cigarettes
betrayed, like strange eyes,
the pontoons orbiting quietly offshore.

A moonlessness gaped beyond
while the frying troughs hissed,
the air rifles snapped,
and the game vendors bellowed,
"Come all!"

Brass fanfare crackled
from stereos on the dark boats
as the first fireworks tore skyward,
as they burned with eagles' screams
and slowed,
as though to gather strength,
before shattering
like gems
against the stars.

Reefer Madness

ALEXA WALKER

Michaela was not one for subtlety. She sucked on a bright-red lolli-pop, her lips wrapping around it to suggest the obvious. Tyler's face remained impassive as he concentrated on Emma Stone shooting at an unfortunate zombie. Her shotgun blew away large chunks of the zombie, body parts and intestines flinging around, which made Tyler internally wince. Ever since the accident, gore disgusted him, but he wasn't going to let Michaela know.

She had been moving slowly into his lap over the course of the night. He felt her snuggle closer into his chest. Tyler sighed. More and more zombies made their way to Emma Stone, their mouths spewing dark blood and snarling for meat. There wasn't any good reason not to reciprocate Michaela's clumsy affections. He felt her breasts push against his chest. Another zombie lost its head, and Tyler felt a cold hand seize his stomach. How disgusting. He stole a glance at Michaela and found her face uncomfortably close to his. She smiled. Her eyes flicked toward his lips. She kissed him.

Tyler gave into it. It was Friday evening. It wasn't like he could go anywhere else.

The local McDonald's was nearly empty. The few customers that populated the place were the ones you'd find at 11:00 p.m. A cop munched on a double-burger in the corner while a young, tattooed couple were feeding each other nuggets on the stools in the center of the restaurant. The cop wore sunglasses, but Tyler had a feeling he was being watched.

"Why don't you just break up with her?" It was a good question. And of course, Frankie would be the one to ask. She wore gear typical of a college athlete: her hair tied up in a loose bun, a red team-issued sweater bearing the school mascot, long black socks, sneakers, the look of exhaustion, and an attitude that told you she didn't give a fuck about it.

He shrugged. "Technically we aren't together."

She pursed her lips. "Well, Michaela thinks you are. How did that happen I wonder?" She turned back to the cashier. "I'll just take a large fry, please." The cashier was a scrawny-looking youth with a nasty wisp of a mustache that he probably thought looked good. Tyler approached him and ordered two burgers, a fry, and a large Coke. The cost ended up being ten dollars and eighty-two cents. Tyler used actual money to pay for it, a ten and a one. When he fished the bills out from his wallet, he glanced very briefly at the picture of the beautiful woman with the loving smile. He quickly shut his wallet.

After receiving their meals and sitting down at a table near the window, Tyler unwrapped his burger. "Have you ever hung out with her?"

Frankie drowned her fries in ketchup before saying, "Not really. I mean, I went to Alpha with her a couple of times freshmen year. We didn't really talk to each other much. I always thought she was kind of annoying."

"Tha's what I'm sa'ing," he said with a mouthful of burger. He took a large gulp from his soda. "Like, she's a total babe or whatever. But she says some stupid shit sometimes. This morning she was talking about how Africans were probably incapable of creating any sort of modern civilization since they were still using spears and wiping their asses with rocks and shit."

"This morning?"

"Like I said, she's a babe."

She made a gagging noise. Tyler smirked. Frankie had been the only friend to last from high school, and he still knew how to push her buttons. She was a serious and mature person. The sort who finishes her homework a week before it's due and the only person who does anything in a group project all while being a starting forward for the soccer team and being a member in campus Bible study. He didn't know how she did it all and still made time for him.

Tyler's phone buzzed.

Packaged deal. Thirty minutes. Brown Ave. You know the place.

Tyler stuffed what remained of his burger into his mouth. "You wa'a go see Jos'ua?"

"What?"

He swallowed. "You want to go see Joshua?"

"I didn't know you still smoked."

"What else can I do in Omaha?"

"You could try to be a productive human being?"

"I'm good."

Frankie took out her keys, which were chained to a golden cross and a rape whistle. Both were given to her by her mother.

"Can I drive?" Tyler asked.

She stared at him.

"Kidding!"

Brown Avenue was known to be the best place to get drugs or mugged. Which one you got was usually up to the coin flip of fate. In the daytime it was completely deserted. But at night, the creepies came out. Dealers. Gang members. Crack addicts. Hookers. Crack-addicted hookers. And Joshua.

Joshua was a pretty good dealer; he was always available, and his prices were fair. But he got super paranoid when he smoked, and he was always smoking. That's part of the reason they usually met behind old buildings in the middle of the night. Joshua also dealt some sketchy stuff, and every once in awhile he would try to convince Tyler to buy. Tyler wasn't that desperate to get that high, and he turned him down every time.

Tyler and Frankie met Joshua behind an old brownstone building that used to be a motel. An old sign that promised clean rooms hung off the front. The ink of the letters trickled downward, like they were bleeding. Joshua was leering about in a worn, brown duffle coat next to his DeLorean, which looked like it had arrived from the '80s without the aid of time travel. He also wore a distinctive green scarf wrapped around his face and shrouding his head. It wasn't really that cold, but Joshua was a weird one.

Frankie snorted, cold fries in hand. "Nice car, McFly."

"Thanks, Jennifer," said Joshua.

"Who?"

"She was Marty's girl in the movies."

"Enough, nerds," Tyler said. "You got the stuff so we can make like trees and get out of here?"

Real potheads know that the way to recognize that your weed is dank, as the kids say nowadays, is by its potent fragrance. "Got you some real good herb, brother." Joshua bent over and held the sack up to Tyler's nose. "Take a whiff."

Tyler didn't even need to sniff. It was so heady that he could smell it outside the sack. "Whoa."

"Yeah, man. Your boy's got you the good stuff."

"Am I going to have to pay extra?" Tyler took the sack and pressed it against his nostrils, taking extreme pleasure in the smell. He offered the sack to Frankie. She just wrinkled her nose.

Joshua shook his head. "Nah, we're good. Consider it a former-athlete's discount."

"Noice." Tyler handed him thirty dollars.

"Much appreciated."

"You wanna smoke with us?"

"Nah, I've gotta go hook another client up." Joshua fist-bumped Tyler. "Maybe next time."

Joshua hopped into his DeLorean and zoomed off. The red back-lights of the car disappeared as it turned onto the street, leaving the two college students alone in the dark alleyway. Tyler checked his phone for the time—11:55 p.m.—then turned to Frankie. "Ready to get fried?"

"Like a potato," she deadpanned.

Tyler took another deep whiff of the fragrance. A lot of people say weed has a skunk-like smell, which in Tyler's opinion was a very unfair comparison by very closed-minded people. Tyler would describe it as simply heavenly, like when you score a winning goal or when you get an A on a test you actually studied for or when you hug your mom again when you've missed her so much. That was what he smelled when he smelled weed—absolute wonder . . . and a hint of fish?

He smelled it again. Yep, that was definitely fish. The scent was faint, hidden underneath the potent odor of the marijuana. He took out his phone, turned on its flashlight, and shone it on the sack. The marijuana inside looked normal; it had a slightly moist and leafy texture. Little crystals sparkled in the light. Again, normal. He examined it closer. Among the clear crystals were traces of red and silver dust. That was definitely not normal. "Fuck."

"What is it?" Frankie asked.

Tyler threw the sack over to her. "That son of a bitch was trying to drug me."

"What? How do you know?" She squinted at the sack. "What's in here?"

He shook his head. "I don't know, some dusty shit." Tyler thought carefully. Joshua had tried to get him to try shrooms, LSD, and co-caine, saying that he knew a guy. But at least then he asked first. "I've told him before. I'm not interested in drugs. Well, not the hard ones."

"Well, I'm sure if you told him 'no,' Joshua isn't going to force you," said Frankie. "He doesn't seem like the type."

He didn't want to admit it at first, but she was right. Joshua was scummy, but not that scummy. "He better not have." Tyler clenched his fist. "If he did I'm going to . . ."

Frankie smirked. "What, roll over his toes?"

Tyler laughed, despite himself.

Frankie tossed back the sack. "Just don't smoke it. Come on, let's go home. I've got practice tomorrow."

Tyler lived on the fifth floor of Parker Hall with a football player. Well, he wasn't a real football player, just an American one. You could pick your own roommate for junior year, but Tyler hadn't had any specific preference and got randomly assigned. Of course, it wasn't really random. That was when Tyler was still an athlete, so he was "randomly" matched with another athlete. Not that he was complaining. Nick Martinez was a nice guy. They actually had a lot in common too. Well, technically only one thing. Pot. But that was enough to establish a friendship.

Tyler rolled into their room, which was more similar to an apartment than a dorm. A pair of cleats and several protective pads were strewn over the couch. Piles of dishes were stacked in the sink. A few socks lay here and there. There was an odd smell of rotten food. Or maybe dirty clothes. Maybe both. A typical room for male athletes. The lights were off, so Nick must have been fast asleep. He probably had early practice tomorrow. Make that today.

Tyler moved quietly into his bedroom. It was decorated with posters of the college soccer team that he couldn't be bothered to take down. The one above his bed was of the whole roster. He was the second on the left, number eleven. The photographer had told the team to force a grimace, but in that moment, all Tyler wanted to do was smile. Tyler ignored it as he prepared to transfer into bed. It was a process he wasn't quite used to. First he had to pull back the sheets and put a pillow in the middle of the bed. Then he could pull himself onto the bed. His arms weren't as beefy as other paraplegics'. Not yet anyway. But he was getting there. It was still very difficult for him to do it. Tyler didn't realize how heavy legs were until he had to lift them himself. He was getting better, though.

He finally managed to get himself into bed in a comfortable position. He closed his eyes and tried to relax. Before the accident, he'd always slept on his stomach. Now he had to sleep on his back. He tried not to think about it. Why he had to literally crawl into bed. Why he was in a wheelchair. Why his mother was dead. But he couldn't help it. How could he? The image would creep into his mind if he let his guard down, even when he was thinking about homework or Michaela or the soccer team. Then there was the crash. And his mother's blood. He really wanted to smoke. *Fucking Joshua and his sketchy-ass goods.*

The next morning, Tyler was awakened by a pounding on his door. He heard Nick's muffled voice. "Tyler?"

He answered, "What?"

"Hey, man," Nick sounded frantic, worried, "you didn't smoke anything yesterday, did you?"

"You can come in, you know," he said, eyes still closed. "And no."

"Oh, good." The door opened. "Tyler, I think something bad happened."

Tyler grunted and looked over to Nick. His blond hair was a mess, and his eyes were unfocused like he'd just smoked a pound of weed. Tyler glanced down at his hands. Nick's left hand was wrapped up in a white towel.

"Dude, I know. Listen, I wasn't careful, and I didn't check it, yeah, but the guy I got it from didn't notice either. No one did."

"Wait. What? What does that mean?"

"Haven't you heard?"

"Heard what?"

"Man, turn on your TV or something. There's some fucked up shit going on."

Luckily, Tyler's dad had set up a TV hanging in the corner of his room. Initially he'd opposed it, saying it made his room look like a hospital. Not that his dad would've listened anyway. He grabbed the remote off his nightstand and flipped it on. The screen flashed to an Asian anchorwoman in a yellow blazer. A flaring red banner read "Pandemic Caused by Marijuana."

"What the fuck?" Tyler turned the volume higher.

"—in the hospital yesterday evening. Symptoms include glazed-over eyes, deadened nervous system, slower brain functions, and intense sensory stimuli. Some patients who have been affected by the disease for a longer period of time may display different symptoms, such as the inability to heal from wounds or enhanced physical abilities. However, sources vary . . ."

"Wait, what makes everyone think that weed caused it?" Tyler asked.

"Man, everyone who was going to the hospital yesterday had smoked too," Nick said.

"That's kind of a stretch, don't you think? Maybe it's just some sort of airborne disease or some shit?"

"Nah, man, I smoked some a couple of days ago." Nick tilted his head. "Or maybe it was a few hours ago."

"And?"

"And I'm still high as a kite, man."

"That's impossible."

"Dude, I'm telling you. I know it sounds crazy but . . . it's different this time. And look. I was trying to slice an apple and nearly chopped my finger off." Nick unwrapped the towel. "Actually, I think I did chop it off." He held a forefinger in his hand. The stub wasn't even bleeding, but the wound was a raw pink. The sight made Tyler retch.

"We need to get you to a hospital," Tyler said as he lifted his covers off.

"You know, when the zombie apocalypse came, I thought it would be more interesting," Tyler said while drinking an Orange-Burst smoothie.

Tyler sat in Groovie-Smoothie on Thirteenth Street and Jackson with Frankie. It was Saturday afternoon. The day was warm and sunny. The aroma of spring filled the air in the form of grassy fragrances and obnoxious humidity. The smoothie bar provided shelter from the heat to many customers. One of them was a zombie. She was standing at the window, staring at the sky. Tyler tried not to stare but couldn't help but glance every once in awhile.

"Did you hear Professor Devon's a zombie?" Frankie asked.

"The guy who teaches metaphysics?" Tyler scoffed. "Doesn't surprise me."

Frankie shook her head. "It's just so crazy. Everything. All of it. Some people are thinking that the zombies are immortal."

"Yeah?"

"The whole team is talking about it," Frankie continued. "Some of the girls have been zombified. They're absolute monsters on the field. Jessica can actually hit the ball into the corners."

"About time." Tyler slurped from his smoothie.

"That's what I thought. I knew she was slow and couldn't control the ball, but she worked her hardest to stay on the team. She came to practice early and stayed after to do her own drills, and she improved! The thing is, even though she can probably score from the middle of the field, she never wants to play. Like I know she can, but she just kind of stands around the field, and you have to yell at her to get her back in the game. And that's when she actually comes to games. I mean, she might be a better player, but her heart's not in it anymore." Frankie cast her eyes downward. "It's like she's a completely different person. She still smiles and makes stupid jokes, but it's not the same. She's just . . . different. Her body's all shriveled, and her teeth look almost greenish. I think her hair's falling out too."

Tyler sat back in his chair and looked again at the zombie girl. She had short hair and a short stature. Her body was thin. Anorexic thin. Her skin was an ugly shade of gray and looked uncomfortably brittle, as if you could peel it back like saran wrap. An untouched blue smoothie stood at her table. He wondered what she was thinking about while gazing up at the sky. Nick had done stuff like that too. Just stare. Sometimes he would stare at the television in their living room or at the lights, with a completely blank expression. It reminded Tyler of that night he was watching *Zombieland* with Michaela. Only without the gore and the blood. The doctors had reattached Nick's finger, but it never healed. Tyler asked Nick once if he was okay with that. He said he was. But his smile was vacant. Tyler wanted to believe him. Maybe Nick had achieved something human beings have been trying to achieve their whole lives. Who was Tyler to doubt it when he was still stuck in a wheelchair?

"You know," he began, "I hear that some zombies who used to be physically disabled are able to get over it after zombificating."

"Yeah, I heard that too." Frankie furrowed her brow in suspicion. "You're not thinking of trying it, are you?"

Tyler pulled at the sleeves of his hoodie. "I still have the grams Joshua gave me. I could smoke it. See what happens."

"I don't know if that's a good idea."

"Why not? I mean it's not like I'm exactly doing well here. I'm stuck in this chair for the rest of my life. My whole life has been soccer until the crash. I don't really know what I want to do with my life."

"You still have school."

"Oh yeah, I'm sure my business degree will get me super far in life, what with the eventual economy crash. Me the paraplegic."

"You can still do things, Tyler."

His eyes started to burn. "Fuck."

Frankie put her hand on his. "Being a zombie isn't the answer. They aren't really alive."

"How do you know that? They seem so much happier than everyone else. Than me."

She bit her lip. "I can't tell you what the right choice is. I don't know if anyone really can. If you think that's the best way, then I can't really stop you. But I don't think it's the right way."

He didn't reply. Frankie grasped his hand. For a moment he didn't reciprocate. Her hand was soft and firm. Tyler looked up into her eyes and saw how intently she looked at him. It struck him how desperate she looked. Like she was trying to convince him to step away from a ledge. Her hand was warm. A weight on his heart he didn't even know that he had was lifted. He closed his fingers around hers.

"Then how will I know what is the right way?" he asked.

She shrugged. "I don't know. I don't know if anyone really does. But that doesn't mean we shouldn't try to figure it out. You have to earn it. You have to win it. It's hard, Tyler, I know, but that doesn't mean you can stop trying. I care about you too much to let you give up. And I'm not going to let go until you know that."

Tyler felt warm tears fall from his eyes and drip down his cheeks. But he found himself smiling still. He squeezed her hand.

The Search for Her

FAITH VICTORIA TRACY

Mind nearly idle, I cast my line,
With it all my unrighteousness.
Through the sapphire, unadulterated pool, it cuts
Agitating the once hushed waters;
Soon, the swells subside
Leaving my speculum clear.
My soul born anew,
Afloat God's Temple,
Drifts with the sanction of Nebraska's Breath
While I wait for sin
And its inescapable tug on my line.
I then smile, for I've found her.

With shined shoes and pressed pants,
I parade with the amiable masses.
Becoming a segment of a barricade,
Painted in professional hues,

I match the Concrete Jungle's pigment perfectly.
Then, while impersonating the architecture
Which surrounds me,
My shoulders kiss strangers.
With each short embrace,
Sweet salutations soon follow
Gently disrupting the compartmentalizations of my life.
I then smile, for I've found her.

As the fatigue seeps from my newly awakened bones,
I plunge my tepid toes into my crumpled, frigid boot.
Then while treading along the beaten, solitary path,
I glance at the still, somnolent sky of stars;
Like precious pearls they gleam illuminating my trail.
Once touched, the gate brands my skin
As I tactfully, cautiously sway it open.
Inside my kind heifer waits;
Her eyes are vigilant, and her bag is packed.
Like lovers with both anxiety and anticipation we wait—
Her for her first and me for my last.
I then smile, for I've found her.

While resting against the enduring, abiding door,
I feel anything but.
My entire entity, esprit, and essence—
Not secured to myself—
Is controlled exclusively by the feverish whims of my precious
    bundle.
My heart does not beat without her heart's permission;
Without her breath, my lungs dare not move.
I linger with hushed lips; for the reassurance
Of her spasmodic kicks and cherished coos, I wait.
Now nodding nearly off, I brush a tiara of unconditional love

Across her barely flushed forehead.
I then smile, for I've found her.

I speak with disjointed syllables
While I listen with foreign ears.
With affable tones,
I am bestowed with hissed and clicked directions.
Once the transparent task is discerned,
I spring into all-consuming action.
My fervid intensity displaying my strong character.
Like the owl, I spend my nights.
Monotonous my duty becomes
Yet my diligence remains uniform.
I am serially searching for the Nebraskan-American Dream.
I then smile, for I've found her.

My heart frantically flutters
As I behold them and all their glory.
These Friday night soldiers in combat
Charge the field of battle.
Concealed beneath bleachers,
I devote myself wholly
To the idolization of every block, pass, and run.
The crowd becomes the infamous Colosseum
Howling overlooked offenses and extolling earned exploits.
As pads collide for the final time,
I wait with caged breath.
I then smile, for I've found her.

With a roar to challenge thunder itself,
We stand united
As a flaming Crimson sea.

For we each have found a personal piece of Nebraskan
    nostalgia:
In the pull of a white bass,
In the face of a once stranger,
In the birth of an innocent calf,
In the break of a persistent fever,
In the promotion of a determined immigrant,
In the touchdown of a Hail Mary,
And in the win of a Husker football game.
We then smile, for we have found her.

The Genuine Effect

BRIAN POMPLUN

My earliest memories are not of arriving but of leaving. Leaving the farm in Elgin, Nebraska, was the thing that I hated most. For a weekend, I was a country kid. A windrower, a cattle herder, a hail driver, and a barn sweeper—the opportunity was limitless. I was an explorer—of woods and fields, machine sheds and garages, haylofts and cellars. I was free.

Then, every trip, Sunday would come. Driving, herding, and exploring were to come to an end. Mom was here. I vividly remember sitting in the backseat, bawling uncontrollably while trying to force my way through the back window and return to the unlimited realm of the rural.

Why did it hurt so badly to leave? It was neither the place nor the endless fun but rather the people. One person in particular mattered above everything else.

Linus John Spieker was a farmer, a father, a Catholic, and an overall wonderful human being. He anchored his family, provided for his community, and left a lasting impression on anyone who met him.

When his memory rises in conversation, everyone smiles. He died three days after my seventh birthday, but in that short time, he showed me how to live. He was my grandfather.

Everything on the farm started early. So early, in fact, that most days the sun had barely taken its blanket off the horizon. I didn't mind. Every minute I could spend awake with him would be the best of the summer.

The breakfasts were hot, hosted in a kitchen strong with the aroma of toast, coffee, and fresh air. Laura, my grandmother, would bustle hurriedly between the appliances, regulating the individual elements of breakfast.

Linus, however, sat placidly at the oval table connected to the island that held the sink. I cannot remember exactly which ones they were, but he would read me comics from the morning paper, and I would laugh. It didn't matter that I didn't understand them; *his* laughter was infectious.

Abruptly, he would rise from the table, go to his room, and in minutes be transformed. Seconds earlier he had been a relaxed soul whose pajamas represented a world of dreams. The embodiment of responsibility and work would return to the kitchen clad in faded blue jeans and a thin flannel shirt over an even more faded undershirt. A ball cap with a thick foam bill and a plastic snap lay tilted over his gray hair. Farmers found this look useful long before hip-hop made it fashionable.

This was always the silent signal for me to don similar "farm clothes" as he made his way outside. One of the rudimentary lessons learned on a farm is that shorts and sandals are inept opponents against thistles and cow shit.

I caught up to him just as he came to the white shed door riddled with chipping paint and guarded by an old seed sign. My cousins have since restored them both. He had a blowtorch in one hand, and the other was throwing a bag of trash into an ancient barrel littered with holes from a thousand burnings. Here, there were no garbage bills.

As the fire ensured that yesterday's belongings returned to dust, he held the shop door, and I scurried inside. Fresh air blended with the aromas of grease, metal, and a dusty concrete floor.

At the time, this shop was my favorite place on Earth. It was an ecosystem all its own, one built by my grandfather. Trucks, tractors, and other vehicles sat to the north. The newest implement took center stage, ready to spring from the east doors. The west wall was dark, piled with objects I still can't define. I didn't get to go back there much.

The south was where we did most of the work. That was where the tools were. The benches. The log holding the nails that each of his grandkids had driven as he taught us to use a hammer. That was where I learned that things in the shop were usually there because they needed to either be mended or blended.

I still marvel at his ability to combine useless objects into functional mechanisms. Things would break, but with his aptitude, they were almost never broken. They had only shifted purpose. His vision taught me to see the possibility in everything. The fan sticks to memory most of all.

It was built of pieces that no one would think could compile into anything useful. Rusted pipes were the body, hinges gave it joints, and an orange power cord coiled its length. It was mobile, attached to the wall somewhere high above the bench on the south side of the shop. A small chain hung just above head level, allowing the fan to be maneuvered wherever he needed to work. Old pieces, retired ones whose courses had long since been run, were brought together to serve another purpose.

Routinely, he would go to the wall and plug in the fan, placing it directly over the section of the bench where he would start working. That morning, however, he stopped short of the bench and instead looked down at me.

"Hop up in the windrower, turn it on, and open the windows," he said with a smile as he held out a single silver key.

It was an ancient machine whose heavy door usually required his hand to open, but adrenaline pulsed through my thumb and directly into the worn chrome button on the handle, popping it open with ease. Everything inside was caked in a layer of dust that felt perfectly in its place. Seasons of cutting field after field of alfalfa had engrained the dusty green smell of summer into the upholstery.

I found the ignition, inserted and turned the key, and felt incredible power as the machine's engine tried to turn over. Startled, I released the key before the engine caught and looked down at my grandfather for reassurance.

"It'll go if you hold on just *this* much longer," he said, laughing and holding his thumb about two inches from his index finger.

Trying again, and holding it just as much as instructed, the motor kicked in. I beamed down at the smiling old farmer. He shook his head, laughing, and waved me back down to the dusty concrete floor.

Maybe he knew it, maybe he didn't, but that simple accomplishment provided me with an understanding of encouragement and trust. I was six. Anyone who trusts a six-year-old with large machinery is either stupid or a very confident educator.

"Let's head to the barn," he said, putting his arm on my shoulder as I returned to ground level. "I want to show you something."

The morning had exploded into its full splendor. Breeze from the cottonwoods carried July snowflakes through the humid air. Moisture from the pasture grass had evaporated, and the blades that had yet to be mowed by the grazing cattle danced. Harsh, angled morning light lit up the red-orange brick of the ranch-style house. The barn across the gravel was a billowing white cloud against an impossibly blue sky.

"What's in the barn?" I asked.

He didn't answer until the giant sliding door had opened and released a cloud of thick dirt that made me cough instantly. He took off his glasses and wiped beads of dirt and sweat from his head with his forearm.

"Have you ever seen an Erin Bird?" he asked, already knowing the answer as I promptly shook my head.

We stepped into the gloomy, stale air, hanging an immediate left into one of the rooms. I walked slowly, allowing my eyes to adjust to the narrow shafts of light coming through streaks in the dirt-stained window. My grandfather had already made his way to the back of the room and withdrew a small object from the freezer. It was wrapped in a shabby old towel.

He met me in the middle of the room and unwrapped the perfectly preserved redheaded woodpecker. "Is that Erin's favorite bird?" I asked, enthusiastically putting the pieces together in my head. Erin is my cousin; growing up in Phoenix, she had been even more deprived than me of the splendors of farm life.

"It is," he said, admiring the natural taxidermy. "Last time she was here, she told me one of her favorite parts of the farm was these birds, and that she wanted to see one up close. So I've been on the lookout for a good one!"

The fact that he had found a dead bird, wrapped it in cloth, and put it in the freezer didn't bother me in the slightest. I was a child. I didn't see any oddity in dead animals yet. I understood a genuine act of kindness from a man who paid attention to somebody else's interests.

Carefully rewrapping the Erin Bird and returning it to its frozen casket, he turned and led me back into the July morning. The temperature was rising quickly. Back at the shop, we climbed into the windrower and headed off to start the day's labor.

We returned exhausted and hungry. I went into the house, shed my boots, and allowed my nose to lead me to the kitchen. My grandmother had already fried the chicken, mashed the potatoes, boiled the corn, and set the table. All I had to do was load up. This was the point in my life when I learned to parallel great food with a long day.

After a quick shower and a change into shorts and a T-shirt, I went back upstairs to find a scoop of ice cream waiting for me atop a slice of peach pie.

"Finish that while I take a shower," he said as he got up. "Then we have a few games of pool to play." His voice carried a hint of challenge as I had beaten him three games to none last night.

The pool table was heavy. I know that because it never moved, and

I had heard, on multiple occasions, how much of a pain-in-the-ass it had been to get down to the basement. It was a dark wood with red felt. A church pew ran alongside it against the pale-green brick wall, seating anyone waiting on the table.

That was where I learned so many things—shot angles from my grandfather and new curse words from my cousins. In the all-too-near-future, it was where the news of his death would reach my ears. It was a place of learning. At the time, it was another of his many classrooms, the kind I didn't want to leave and couldn't help but pay attention in.

I played with a small cue he had fashioned to fit his growing grandchildren. That evening, he returned the favor I had given the night before and beat me three games to none. I had taken a few shots that I knew to be difficult, and none of them ended well for me. I sat on the church pew and pouted into my root beer.

"If I had made that last shot, I would have won for sure," I said with a hopeless confidence.

Ending the night with his best lesson to date, he replied, "*If* is a small word that has the biggest meaning."

Even today, those words find their way into every decision I make. How will *this* affect *that*? Find the *if* and weigh the options.

I still miss the farm, the adventure, and gaining the invaluable wisdom of a genuine person. I wonder what things I haven't learned yet and how I can relay what he taught me. Whenever these thoughts work their way through my head, I smile because I always come to the same conclusion. It takes a good person to be truly happy, and I was blessed with one of the most qualified instructors.

Release

KRISTI WALSH

Panel-selected prize winner in fiction

My father's sister Rachel was nothing like him. I'd only lived with her and her family for two weeks, but the adjustment had been less than smooth. Aunt Lil, my mother's sister, and I had had our easy peace for the previous five years, going about our own lives and passing back and forth a few times a week, and before that my parents were so far from ordinary that there was barely any point in pretending to be a real family.

But at Rachel's, it was messily painted pictures on the fridge, posed photos lining the staircase, everyone at the dinner table every night. Usually it was something Rachel had made herself—I hadn't seen a microwavable meal since I got there. I could barely believe I was related to them. Or, really, that Jonathan was related to them.

Rachel had made a full breakfast of pancakes and bacon for the whole family, a picture of true Americana. I was avoiding the sight of syrup dripping from little Mikey's missing-teeth mouth while

Rachel flipped through the mail. Her voice, already squeaky, seemed an octave higher, and her movements were far too shaky. Something was up.

"The breast cancer charity wants money again . . . something from the elementary school . . . the water bill . . . oh, Jess, you got a letter."

My blood seemed to drop ten degrees. I froze in place.

"A letter?" Arthur asked me, seemingly oblivious to his wife's odd voice. "One of your old friends? From Omaha?"

If I had been any more coherent, I might have snorted. No one sent snail mail anymore, unless they had no other way to communicate.

For example, prison inmates.

Rachel looked at him with raised, perfectly plucked eyebrows. "No. From Jonathan."

"I don't want it," I said. The words felt like sandpaper, came out like a croak.

Rachel looked up sharply. "Jessica."

"No. Seriously. I don't want it."

Breakfast completely slowed to a halt. My oldest cousin, Audrey, watched with interested eyes. Mikey ping-ponged back and forth between Rachel and me. Even Arthur stopped chewing.

Rachel scrunched her nose and eyebrows closer together, like the words were caught in her mouth. Finally, she decided on what she wanted to say. "Jess, he really cares about you."

A million responses zipped through my head. *He could have shown it better. He said he really cared about my mom too. If he'd really loved me, he would have been a good husband and father.*

None of those responses came out of my mouth. What did pop out was, "Fuck him."

Rachel gasped, her hands coming up over her mouth like in an old-fashioned movie. Rather than sticking around to be scolded for my language, I stood up, walked to the back door, snagged my key off the hook, and went to my car. Didn't matter where I went, but I couldn't be there anymore. Not for today.

Monday morning dawned bright and clear, and I was glad to get back into the routine of school. Rachel and Arthur hadn't said anything when I came back to the house, maybe because I was only gone for an hour, but the awkwardness had lingered in the air for the rest of the weekend, and I had overheard Arthur talking to Mikey about how sometimes grown-ups used bad words that kids weren't allowed to say yet. I really sucked at this whole pseudo older sister thing.

I pulled my math book out of my backpack and flipped to where I had left my homework neatly pressed between the pages the night before. Only instead of seeing the college-ruled loose-leaf paper filled with equations, a handwritten letter lay there too.

Without even meaning to, I scanned the few lines.

Dear Jessie,

Rachel told me you've moved to Hastings to stay with her. I'm very sorry to hear about Lillian—I know the two of you were close.

Jessie, I know we haven't talked for years, but I would really like to see you. This Saturday is a visit day at the prison. I don't expect you to come, but I would truly love it if you did.

Love always,
Dad

I jumped up, crumpling the letter and my homework together in my hand. The world spun, the whiteboard rocking back and forth as if it were on a seesaw. I blinked at Miss Davis, who was eyeing me with concern. Her light-brown hair swam in front of my face, becoming darker . . . her face more angular . . . her throat, her chest, her stomach soaked in deep-red blood, the kind that kills. I pictured an emerald necklace dangling broken on the ground, torn roughly from her neck in her final moments. I blinked again. Miss Davis returned.

"I'm going to . . . go to the nurse's office," I blurted, the words falling out. I tried to run out of the room, but it was like my feet were concrete blocks, tripping me. I managed to stay upright and staggered my way into the nearest girl's bathroom, which was empty, thank God. It had been years since I had cried in a bathroom stall—I'd stopped that soon after I had moved into my Omaha middle school.

I leaned over the toilet, heaving, waiting to see if I would throw up. After a minute, the bile seemed to recede, coiling into a pit in my stomach, and I felt confident enough to straighten up and lean against the stall door. The ringing in my ears dulled slightly.

"I'm sorry he said that to you," Aunt Lil had said, back when I was eleven and having my first ever panic attack after he'd tried to claim his innocence in a letter to me. After that, with my permission, she used to throw away the letters and not even tell me that they'd come, and I had tried to fool myself into believing that they didn't exist. That he didn't exist.

But he did exist. And he wanted to see me.

Well, of course he did. Maybe he wanted to protest his innocence, like he had throughout the entire trial. Maybe he wanted forgiveness—*Hey, sorry I murdered your mother. See you at Christmas?* Maybe—

I would never know what he wanted unless I talked with him.

"You had no right."

Rachel looked up from her cutting board as I stormed through the kitchen door, a few thin slices of celery sticking to her knife. "What's that?"

Even without knowing her too well, I could see through her. "Putting that letter there. I told you I didn't want it."

"Jess, please just listen to me. He's your father. He loves you."

"Bullshit. Absolute bullshit. You don't get to decide anything, Rachel. That man isn't my dad. He quit being my dad when he killed my mom."

"Allegedly."

"Bullshit allegedly! He fucking did it! He was convicted!"

"*Jess!* Language!"

"Aunt Rachel, so help me God, you better not give me another letter from Jonathan. Ever." I stormed up the stairs and slammed my bedroom door.

I had to go through the metal detector twice. Not because I forgot something the first time but because I chickened out and had to go back outside to breathe. It didn't help much. When they escorted me to my booth, I felt like the prison guard was my waiter, only instead of delivering a meal to a customer, she was delivering me to a murderer.

I sat and looked at him through the clear Plexiglas window. His head hung low, chin nearly touching his chest, not making eye contact.

I waited for him to make the first move. He was the one who wanted to talk to me, after all.

He picked up the phone, a black pay phone–type like they always had in movies. Then he looked up sharply, almost as if he had choreographed it.

His clear blue eyes met my own, and I was uncomfortably reminded of how similar our eyes were. We once shared white-blond hair, but mine had been L'Oréal Medium Chocolate for years. My contacts hid our shared nearsightedness. We used to have similar freckles, but now he sported a ghostly prison pallor. But underneath it all were our pointy noses, our tiny ears, our deep-set eyes. I couldn't change our features.

"You look so much like Jonathan," Rachel had said to me when she had picked me up from the airport. It was easier to believe she was making things up when the proof wasn't on the other side of a table from me.

I picked up my own phone. The plastic was cold against my skin, particularly compared to the hot room. I was baking in my sweater. Or maybe I was just warm, in general. My blood was racing.

"Hi, Jessie," my father said from the other side. His voice was hoarser than I remembered. "Thanks for coming."

"All rise for the Honorable Judge Catherine Richards."

Five years previously. I was twelve and even more lost than most other kids my age. I couldn't decide if I felt incredibly old or young. Some days, like when Aunt Lil brought me a box of family heirlooms and I had to help decide who to disperse them to, I felt older, mature, a trusted voice in answering the question *What would Sal have wanted?*

Other days, like when the judge awarded Aunt Lil full custody of me, without even asking me where I wanted to live, I felt like a stupid child, left to be divvied up like Mom's clothes or books or jewelry. I was waved out of the room while Aunt Lil talked with the other relatives about how the trial was going, no matter how much I protested. Aunt Lil made all the funeral arrangements without ever asking me what I wanted, not that I would have had any clue at all.

My father was led in by the bailiff, the one with the massive shaved head and slightly too-short uniform pants. By contrast, my father seemed to be drowning in his orange jumpsuit, small and reedy, white-blond hair flopping into his eyes like an overgrown teenager.

I couldn't stop staring at him. At the way he didn't look at anyone, not even me. At the way his gait was fast and jerky, and I couldn't tell if that was a new tic or something I had just never noticed before. Most of all, at the way he seemed to shrink into the wooden chair. He was handcuffed and didn't seem to mind, twisting his fingers into grotesque shapes in the sort of coping mechanism he had adopted soon after being arrested. I felt Lil stiffen up beside me.

The very air itself seemed anxious.

The jury foreman wore a green button-down shirt and khaki pants. The colors made me think of the Crocodile Hunter.

"How does the jury find?"

"The jury finds the defendant," a pause, "guilty."

Lil exhaled and closed her eyes. A few rows away, Rachel burst into loud, wailing tears. I didn't know what to do, so I just put my head in my lap and breathed, like the stupid therapist Lil had gotten for me had recommended.

Jonathan was the only one who didn't react.

"I didn't want to come," I told him. Honestly.

His mouth twisted, just like Rachel's always did. He looked genuinely regretful, with turned-down eyes and a mouth like a puppy. I almost believed it. "Really? You weren't curious about me at all?"

"No."

"Oh." He leaned onto the side of the wall where the phone hung, as if he weren't strong enough to stay sitting upright. "I've been curious about you."

I felt a tiny flicker in my stomach and trapped it down. I didn't want to be happy that he was still thinking about me.

Fifth grade. A year before my mother died.

"Jessie's dance recital is this Sunday," my mom said hesitantly. I stopped before I went into the kitchen and pressed myself against the wall. I would get in trouble if they caught me eavesdropping.

"Yeah." It wasn't a question, but it also wasn't a statement of knowledge.

"Are you going to go?"

The click of a cigarette lighter. My father always made a point to smoke inside the house when he was pissed at my asthmatic mother.

"I don't give a flying fuck about it," he said. I winced. I hated it when my dad cursed.

The sound of a breath—my mother screwing up what was left of her shattered courage. "It would be really nice if you went. You've missed the last two. All the other girls' dads come."

A sharp smack from the kitchen. I brought my hand to my face, nervously chewing the ruffles on the sleeve of my nightgown.

"I said I didn't give a flying fuck," he said.

"What do you want?" I asked.

He looked offended, and again I almost believed it. "To see you. You're my daughter."

"If you hadn't killed Mom, you could see me every day," I said, then sucked in a breath. I hadn't meant to say that. I had intended to find out what he wanted, maybe put some demons to rest, and to not rise to his bait.

Clearly, that wasn't happening like I had planned.

That Sunday he showed up late to the recital, missing my dance completely but bringing along a bouquet bigger than any of the other girls ever got from their own dads. My mom wore her sunglasses throughout the recital.

"But here's the thing," he said. "I didn't kill your mother."

The bile already growing in my stomach rose to my throat. I tried to open my mouth, but I had to close it.

"I know you don't believe me," he said. "And you know, I get why you wouldn't. But I didn't do it, and even if the damn court didn't believe me, I want you to."

Third grade. Every Thursday a kid's parent would come in and tell the class about their job and bring a snack.

My mother didn't want to go in. "Honey, I just do a lot of boring paperwork at home. Can't you ask your teacher if she can skip you?"

"What about me?" my dad asked. His voice was soft, but the good kind of soft, not his dangerous voice.

My mom fiddled with the pendant on her emerald necklace. "Well, honey," she said. "You sell furniture. What can you do with that?"

"I'll do something fun," Dad said. "Come on, Sal. You can't tell her teacher her parents won't come in."

Wednesday night, my parents got into a fight. Not their worst by a long shot but bad enough that I spent all evening in my room, eating from a box of cereal I hid under the bed for occasions like that. They didn't get to blows, though, so I considered it a victory.

I spent all Thursday terrified. What if Dad didn't show up? Worse than that, what if he did, and he yelled at me in front of the class like he had yelled at me to go upstairs the day before?

And then he walked in, his face all lit up, holding a cardboard box full of surprises. He passed out paint chips, collected ideas for furniture the company could make next (including triple-decker bunk beds), and told a funny story about a husband and wife who got two halves of a couch when they couldn't decide which one to buy. Somehow, he made being a furniture salesman seem like being a circus clown.

I looked around the room, watching my classmates stare at this man. He could absolutely enthrall a crowd, whether they were a group of eight-year-olds or a couple of customers deciding on a recliner. For the first time in my life, I wanted to stand up next to him and exclaim, "That's my dad!"

As the class packed up, I listened over the din as he thanked my teacher.

"That was a great presentation," Mrs. Grondowski said to him. "Jessie must be so proud. She's a sweetheart."

I could hear the smile in my dad's response, the pride leaking out into his words. "She's the best part of my life."

I tried to open my mouth again.

"I loved your mother. And I love you," he said. "I get I might have had a . . . rough way of showing it, but you have to believe me."

Don't ask it, I heard Aunt Lil's voice in my head. *Walk away, right now.*

"Why? Why should I believe you?"

He leaned in close to me. "Because you and I both know that I didn't. You just don't want to admit it to yourself. I never wanted your mother dead."

And there it was. The truth.

"Is Daddy coming home tonight?" I asked my mom as we lay on our backs, our heads underneath the Christmas tree.

"Mmm, we'll see," she said.

My little heart leapt. Christmas without Dad could be really nice. Last year Dad and Mommy had gotten into a huge fight, and Mommy sent me away, and I didn't open my present until two days later. This could be better.

"Where does he go? When he's not at work?" I asked.

My mom raised her eyebrows. A tiny scar, courtesy of the downstairs bathroom door frame, bisected her left one.

"He's with Holly," she said.

"Like the stuff on the wreath?"

She smiled at me, warm and bright like the tree above us. "Sure, honey."

"Yeah, I lost my temper sometimes," he said. "But never that hard, you know? How does someone go from maybe—I'll admit it, I'm a big enough person—making a bad choice and smacking someone every once in awhile to full on murder? And the person who killed her tore off the necklace, and you and I both know I would never have done that. I am *enraged* that someone would do that."

The key little fact that had bothered me ever since the police arrested Jonathan. The stupid emerald necklace. He treated it like a branding. There's no way that he would ever take it off her.

Get out of here. Don't listen to this anymore, Aunt Lil's voice said again.

This time I listened to her. "I don't need to hear this. I'm leaving," I said. "And I'm never coming back." I stood up from the seat, noticing for the first time how my knees ached. I had been tenser than I had thought.

"That's what you said last time. Six years ago. And look where you are."

Compared to the sickly, listing prisoner I'd encountered when I walked in, my father now stood proud like a king.

Aunt Lil had loved me, a lot, but didn't really know what to do with me. She had been a professor of medieval literature at the University of Nebraska–Omaha, renowned in her field. When I was little, I always got packages in the mail from her. Nesting dolls from Russia, a beaded necklace from Turkey, a hand-carved statue from Indonesia. I would go years seeing her only at Christmas, but she talked to my mother on the phone every day when my father was at work and couldn't listen in. She was so fiercely independent that she didn't tell me she had ovarian cancer until it was already terminal.

I asked my mom once why I had cousins on my dad's side but not hers.

"Oh, sweetie," she said. "Your aunt Lil is too exciting to settle down. Some people are meant to live in a little house with their family, and some people want to see everything that there is to see. That's why I get to live here, with you, and she goes all over the place."

When Mom died, there wasn't much of a question where I would go. It was between Aunt Rachel, my father's sister, and my mom's sister Aunt Lillian. Aunt Lil was single with a decent job, an extra bedroom, and a fierce determination that I would never contact Jonathan Arnold again. Aunt Rachel had a tiny house, was pregnant with her fourth child, and shared DNA with the man who had murdered my mother. I moved to Omaha right after my mother was buried.

Aunt Lil barely changed her schedule when I moved in. The university where she taught was a forty-minute commute for her, and with her full load of classes, I spent a lot of time on my own. I didn't really mind, though. Much as I admired Aunt Lil, living with her scared me for the first few years.

Once, about a month after I moved in, I accidentally kicked the small stack of mail that had landed on the entryway rug.

Bills (one from the funeral home), a few sympathy cards for her, and a letter addressed to me. Maybe it was one of my old friends reaching out. I hadn't heard from any of them since my father's face was plastered on every news station in Nebraska.

I ripped it open.

Dear Jessie,

I'm just writing to tell you that you can't believe what everyone is saying. I know you know that I could never have hurt your mother like this. I love her—and you—very much. So long as you remember this, I am okay to live in this prison.

Love,
Daddy

Aunt Lil came home an hour later to find me huddled in the corner of the hallway bathroom, still shaking. The letter lay trampled at my feet.

"Don't worry," she said. "He is never, ever going to get out of prison. And he is never, ever going to talk to you again—and you shouldn't contact him either."

I wished I had just listened to her then.

The office of Hadley, Rogers, and Sternum, Attorneys at Law, looked exactly as intimidating as I had always pictured a snooty defense office to be. That is, if I'd spent much time picturing them.

Samuel Rogers had his name splashed everywhere in his office: printed on diplomas hanging from the dark oak paneling, engraved in the golden pen displayed on his desk (clearly this wasn't the type of man who used Bic or Paper Mate), and prominently embossed in the letterhead of his stationery. He had a little mustache that was probably once as dark as his walls but was fading into something closer to the color of the pen. He crossed his legs, and his dark suit pants lifted enough to fully expose his expensive leather shoes.

Sitting in the cushy chair across from him, my sneakered foot shaking up and down faster than my heartbeat, I'd never felt so underdressed.

Rogers was kindly pretending not to notice that I was in jeans and a zip-up hoodie. He leaned back in his chair. "I hadn't heard from

Charlene Montgomery in years. I was surprised when she asked me to take on this case."

"I had to pull in a lot of favors," I said, not wanting to remember the Monday before, when I'd brought a pile of public-record papers and a typed list of all my questions to Patrick Montgomery, a kid in my history class, and literally begged him on my knees to bring it to his attorney mother. It was possibly the most embarrassing thing I had done since I had moved to Hastings, and that was saying something.

He nodded. "I didn't expect to be interested in it—but it did catch my attention. Enough to call you in."

"So they really didn't have a case against him?" I asked. I didn't know how much this guy was going to cost, but if I had to pay by the hour, he needed to hurry it up.

He shrugged. "I mean, not an airtight case, but it was okay. Maybe a better defense could have gotten him off, maybe not. But the DA definitely had enough to prosecute."

"But they didn't have anything on him!"

He closed his eyes. "Look, kid. They had a lot more than a lot of cases. Let me guess—you watch a lot of *CSI*? *Law and Order*?"

My spine straightened at being addressed as "kid." "I was kind of turned off from crime shows at an early age," I said. I heard the bite in my tone and made no real effort to hold it back.

He shrugged. "Fair enough. But most cases don't have physical evidence. It's *hard* to get usable DNA and even harder to get a fingerprint. And even if they did, your dad wasn't in the system. They couldn't have matched the murder weapon to him, even if they had it."

"So what did they have?"

He shuffled the papers. "A forensic psychologist testified about the kind of person who would commit this crime—sociopathic, narcissistic, violent. And then he talked about interviews he'd had with your dad and people around your dad—his coworkers, his family, including you. And then he testified that your dad fit the type of personality who would commit this crime."

All of a sudden, a memory I didn't know I had: sitting in a too-warm office surrounded by dolls and stuffed animals and diplomas on the wall, and a man with a sailboat tie asking me to tell him about my dad. I felt cold.

"Okay," I said. "So what else?"

"The medical examiner said that judging by the angle and the strength of the stab wounds, the murderer was between five-eight and six feet tall, weighed 160 to 180 pounds, and was most likely a male. Jonathan fit that description."

"So does my friend. And my uncle. And my history teacher."

"People testified about his abuse. You. Lillian. The DA even got your aunt Rachel to admit that he wasn't a good guy. The jury was incredibly sympathetic."

"But that doesn't prove he killed her."

"I know. But a lot of the time, it doesn't actually work like innocent until proven guilty. Your father was a proven asshole who was proven to, on occasion, physically attack your mom. And the stinger was that his alibi totally fell through. He said he was with Holly Garlowe in the office late that night. Holly Garlowe denied having anything but the most professional relationship with him and said that she hadn't seen him since she'd left work at noon that day."

"But she was lying," I said. "She was covering up for her husband. Who also fits the description. Five-nine. No alibi. Violent."

"Right, but no one was looking at him. Why would they? No one thought Henry Garlowe even knew Sally Arnold, much less had a reason to kill her."

I ground my teeth. "Except the fucking lead detective."

Rogers smiled slightly, a grim little uplifting of the corners of his mouth. "Right. Frankly, I don't know how that didn't get caught. The lead detective being related to the husband of a key witness absolutely should have been brought up. But they didn't have the same last name, weren't legally anything. It was an oversight. I'd love to tell you that oversights never happen, but as a defense attorney they're my bread and butter. And that quack of an attorney your aunt hired . . . he must have been a real idiot. Probably not Elle Woods quality."

I blinked.

"It's a joke, sweetie."

"Right." I took a deep breath. "So—so what does this mean?"

He leaned forward on his desk, pulling his jacket sleeves down to expose his monogrammed cuff links. SMR. I wondered what his middle name was. Michael? Matthew?

"It means that, with this out, I can argue for a mistrial. It's called a Brady violation. Basically, your father got unfair representation due to the detective not following due process. I could go into a lot more detail than that, but that would just take up more time, and you don't seem like you can afford me that well to begin with."

I sat up straighter. "What will happen with a mistrial?"

"He'll get a new trial. Same charges, the DA's office, and whoever your father's defense attorney is. I would be willing to take that additional case on, if you wanted, but I don't think that will be necessary."

"Why not?"

"Because my guess is, instead of charging him again, they'll drop the charges. If the DA has enough evidence against Henry Garlowe, they may press charges against him—that's totally out of my control. But in any case, with a plausible second candidate for the crime, a competent lawyer can shred the circumstantial evidence to pieces. He wouldn't be convicted in a new trial. The DA would probably just let him go."

My heart thumped a little harder in my chest. "So if I decide to hire you—"

"Then I submit an appeal citing the lead detective's incompetence, and we go to court to declare a mistrial. We go again to see if the DA will press charges again against Jonathan. In the unlikely case that they do, the murder trial starts all over again. If they do not press charges, Jonathan Arnold will walk out a free man."

Free.

I pictured Jonathan walking around. For some reason, I pictured him swinging his arms and whistling like a cartoon character. My mental picture of him was wearing the stupid orange jumpsuit. I couldn't even remember the clothes he used to wear.

I sat on my hands to stop the shaking.

"And how much do you cost?" I asked. I was aiming for professional, but my voice wobbled a bit.

He gave that grim little smile again, and he told me.

I choked. Not only was it going to be all of my inheritance from Aunt Lil, it still wouldn't be enough—and I knew Aunt Lil would rather die all over again than let any of her money go to freeing Jonathan. But then I remembered Rachel. She had paid for the attorney the first time and apparently hadn't had enough to hire a good one, but if she helped me out, maybe we could afford this Samuel M. Rogers.

College flashed in front of me. A dorm room of my own, blessedly free from Mikey's toys spread across the floor like a death trap and Missy's piles of clothes on the bathroom floor.

How the hell could I afford that if I spent all my money getting Jonathan out?

And if he got out, what the hell was he going to do?

When I was thirteen, I accidentally overheard Aunt Lil on the phone with one of the law professors at her university.

"So, if this is an appeal, what chance does he have of getting out?" she said, pacing back and forth across the kitchen floor. This is where my mom and aunt were different. My mother was slower, more beaten down. When things got bad, she withdrew into herself, like it took all her energy to keep breathing. When Lillian was stressed, she became a fireball of energy, which crackled all around her. She could never stop moving.

Apparently the voice on the other line hadn't appeased her. "I just want him to rot in jail and then rot in hell," she said, running her hands through her hair, which had grayed so much in the past year.

"Honestly I would have said that even before the—the murder. How he treated her was absolutely *criminal.*"

But he was innocent. Well, guilty enough—of hurting my mom, physically and emotionally, of cheating on her, of just being an asshole. But he hadn't wanted her dead.

Was it really fair if he spent the rest of his life in prison for someone else's choice?

"I'll hire you," I said to Samuel M. Rogers. "I'll make sure you get paid. But get him free."

Behind my eyelids, I could see Aunt Lil tearing up with relief when the jury foreman pronounced my father guilty. I had never felt so horrible in my life.

Six months feels like forever when you're waiting for trial paperwork and appeals and lawyers and signed documents, and your dead aunt is constantly crying in your head every time you close your eyes. But apparently it is lightning speed in terms of the legal system.

That following May, I stood outside under the clear, cloudless sun and watched my father walk out of the state penitentiary wearing the jeans and button-up shirt that Aunt Rachel had bought him. Unlike my mental image, he wasn't skipping and whistling.

Aunt Rachel cried on the spot, just like I expected. "I can't believe it finally happened," she said, her voice muffled. "And it's all thanks to Jess. She's the one who did *everything.*" This was not news to my father. Aunt Lil started screaming in my head.

I had to stop her. I couldn't leave Aunt Lil like that. I held up my hand to stop him from reaching in for the hug.

"Look," I said. "If the best thing you can say for yourself as a father is that you didn't personally kill my mother, you've really fucked up. And you're right. If you didn't kill her, you deserve to be free. But that doesn't mean you can rewind six years and pretend you were there. It doesn't mean you can go back the eleven years before that and say you were a good dad. Because the truth is, you sucked. You were awful. So you weren't a dad then, and you don't get to be one now."

He opened his mouth, his weak chin trembling. I felt no pity.

"So you can be free. But so help me God, if you ever try to talk to me again, or if you conspire with Rachel so that we meet up, or anything like that, I will get a restraining order. And if you violate that, I will kill you and claim self-defense. And you know I'll win." I stared straight into his eyes. Blue, like my own.

"Goodbye, Jonathan."

In the back of my head, Lillian choked back a sob and, for a second, stopped crying.

There Is No Place Like Nebraska

ELLIE FEIS

There Is No Place Like Nebraska. Go Big Red. Husker Power. Although I was born and raised in Sacramento, California, I've known these sayings for as long as I can remember. My father was born in Franklin, Nebraska, and even though he moved out of state at an early age, he never loved any other place in the world as much as he loved Nebraska. It was his goal to create the next generation of Husker fans out of me and my siblings. I had a Nebraska cheerleading uniform. He covered my brother's room with posters of Memorial Stadium. And before I was even eleven years old, I had taken three road trips from California to Nebraska.

"Our family is a Nebraska family," my dad would always say with pride. And I absolutely hated it.

I can't remember the exact moment I started to loathe Nebraska. Maybe it was because Saturdays usually meant watching the Cornhuskers play. Maybe it was because most conversations with my dad's family revolved around Husker football. Maybe it was due to my mom's belief that Nebraska was God's gift to the United States of America, even though she'd never lived there herself. Or maybe it was because I grew up listening to what felt like a never-ending list detailing how Nebraska was superior to California. All I know is at some point, I couldn't tolerate anything about Nebraska. If the Huskers were playing, I shut myself away in my room. If my family talked about football, I ignored them. And for the most part, I succeeded in forgetting the state even existed.

Then 2010 happened.

My oldest sister, Beth, graduated high school and announced that she was going to attend the University of Nebraska–Lincoln. I thought she was insane. I found a sick form of satisfaction in thinking that when she moved away she would eventually realize how awful Nebraska actually was and would decide to come home.

I was wrong.

During winter break, she couldn't stop telling us stories about how amazing Nebraska was. Everyone was so nice. There was snow. Husker game days were unbelievable. She was learning so much. The list dragged on and on. She didn't even want to be home. She wanted to go back to her Nebraska life as soon as possible.

I decided she was a lost cause; there was no saving her. To this day she lives in Nebraska.

My mom, my sister Becky, and I went on a road trip during spring break of my freshman year of high school to visit Beth. During the trip, Becky too became infected with a love for Nebraska. By the time we were getting ready to go on the same road trip a year later, Becky had done the unspeakable and decided to go to Nebraska for school. Another one of my sisters was lost.

Well, it wasn't going to happen to me. No way. My rebellion grew stronger and stronger, and I spent more and more of my time looking at other schools. Although I enjoyed visiting over spring break, I was determined to make my own path. People who asked me where I wanted to go to school always received the same reply.

Anywhere but Nebraska.

The next year, my junior year, we made our annual trip out to

Nebraska, and this time Becky showed me the UNL campus and let me stay with her a night in the dorms. It was one of the most fun experiences of my entire life. But I still couldn't let myself love Nebraska. During my senior year of high school, I chose the University of Minnesota as my number one college. Nebraska was on the bottom of my list.

Everything about Minnesota was perfect on paper. There were many factors about Minnesota that I liked—good academics, good location, professional sports teams—but the best part of Minnesota was that it was definitely *not* Nebraska.

"Who knows? Maybe this time next year you might have a Minnesota sweatshirt," I told my dad one day, just to see his reaction.

"You couldn't pay me to wear it." Needless to say, my dad didn't talk to me that much during that stage in my life. He loved me, but he also loved Nebraska. To say that I was breaking his heart would be an understatement.

In February of 2014, my mom and I flew to Minneapolis to go on a campus tour of the University of Minnesota. I remember believing I was making my first visit to the city I would be living in for the next four years.

And boy, was I wrong.

Before the trip, I was so ready to tell everyone I was going to Minnesota for school. And yet, I couldn't confirm my enrollment after my tour. Everything I had reasoned before about why Minnesota was perfect didn't work anymore. Something just wasn't right.

And then I realized the reason I thought Minnesota was perfect was the exact same reason I couldn't go there.

It wasn't Nebraska.

Every school I thought I would go to before Nebraska had something missing, something that made me feel like going there would be a mistake. I had to do some soul-searching. If I went to any other place than Nebraska for school, I would spend my entire life wondering "what if." I knew I would miss out on an incredible experience in an incredible state if I went anywhere else for school. I would be left out of amazing traditions and a state pride that didn't exist anywhere else in the world. Even though I hadn't realized it, I had fallen in love with Nebraska. And so, I swallowed my pride.

I get asked all the time why I chose to leave California to live in Nebraska. I have a list of reasons I always say—I grew up in a Husker household, I have relatives here, my older sisters went here for school—but the real reason I became a Husker is because I realized you can search everywhere for a place like Nebraska, but you'll never find it.

Because there really *is* no place like Nebraska.

CONTRIBUTORS

BRIANNA AGUILAR graduated from Grand Island Senior High in May 2016. She is planning to major in nursing at Bryan College of Health Sciences in Lincoln, Nebraska. Her essay was originally written for a class assignment. She enjoyed learning about the history of her country and about the history of her family and how they originated in the United States, especially hearing all of the details from her grandpa. Her family members have lived in Grand Island since their arrival in America, and they absolutely love Nebraska.

KAMRIN BAKER is a senior at Miller West High School, a contributor for the teen section of the *Huffington Post*, and an editorial writer for *Local Wolves Magazine*. She loves dogs and ranch dressing and perpetually quotes Taylor Swift in social situations. She plans to major in print journalism.

LANE CHASEK was born in Chadron, Nebraska, and is currently an English major at the University of Nebraska–Lincoln. He has previously published poems in *Laurus*.

ASHLEY LYNNE COOK was born along with her twin sister, Amanda, on a cold and snowy morning, February 5, 1998, in Rothenberg, Germany. With her father in the military, the family of six moved from country to country, state to state. After twenty-one years of being in the military, her father decided to retire, landing them back with her parents' roots in Nebraska. After spending four years going to Waverly High School, her love of sports, books, and art grew. Whenever they can, she and her family visit relatives in Brainard. Helping with whatever her grandparents and uncles need, she gets the taste of Nebraska farm life.

RACHEL DANIELSON is a high school senior from Gibbon, Nebraska. She grew up in the heart of the Platte River valley.

BRIANA DAVIS is an occupational therapy student at the College of Saint Mary in Omaha. She has always enjoyed writing and connecting personal stories to other events. Her hobbies include running, baking, and helping on the family farm.

ELLIE FEIS is a sophomore advertising/public relations and English major at the University of Nebraska–Lincoln. She loves reading, writing, and drinking coffee. She is from Sacramento, California, and she has two older sisters and a younger brother. She has an unhealthy obsession with pizza and watching movies.

LUKE GILBERT

NINA HJERMSTAD is from the small town of Louisville, Nebraska, where she received a huge amount of support for her creative writing in high school. Since coming to the University of Nebraska–Lincoln, she has been pleasantly surprised to find the same kind of attentiveness and support that she found in her small community at home. In addition to her love of writing, she is an avid reader, roller derby player, crafter, and animal cuddler.

AMANDA HOVSETH was born and raised in Scottsbluff, Nebraska. She is a senior at the University of Nebraska–Lincoln, where she is studying English with a focus on creative writing. *Perspective: A Dark Tale of Hope* is the title of her previously published novel. She is currently in the process of opening her own publishing company called Synecdoche Publishing LLC.

DANIEL MCILHON is an undergraduate student at Creighton University, pursuing bachelor's degrees in English and theology. He enjoys, among other things, border collies, pine-scented soaps, and brevity. He lives in Des Moines, Iowa, with his zero border collies.

SARA MOSIER is a Lincoln, Nebraska, native and a senior at the University of Nebraska–Lincoln, studying English with a focus on creative writing. She plans to graduate in 2016 with her bachelor's degree. She is an award-winning photographer for *Laurus* magazine at UNL, and her photography and poetry have been published in several other literary magazines.

CATHERINE PEDIGO is a student at Creighton University in Omaha, Nebraska.

BRIAN POMPLUN studies secondary language arts education at the University of Nebraska–Omaha. He grew up as a "town kid" in Fullerton, Nebraska, and was always (and remains) attracted to the lifestyle of rural Nebraska. Since high school, he has lived in both Lincoln and Omaha and studied various styles of art, including photography, graphic design, and creative nonfiction writing. He enjoys traveling with his wife.

THADDEUS SIMPSON has lived in Nebraska since he was three. He enjoys reading, writing, the Nebraska summertime, and practicing his nunchuck skills.

FAITH VICTORIA TRACY

ALEXIS VRANA is a senior at Wahoo High School. She loves to golf. She has golfed all four years of her high school career, and her team has made it to state twice. She enjoys playing in the Wahoo High School band.

ALEXA WALKER is a student at Creighton University majoring in English.

KRISTI WALSH is a senior English major at Creighton University, where she also studies technical theater.

CPSIA information can be obtained
at www.ICGtesting.com
Printed in the USA
LVOW03s1908030417
529446LV00001B/164/P